walking easy

in the

Swiss Alps

Chet & Carolee Lipton

GATEWAY
BOOKS

Printed in the United States of America

Gateway Books
San Rafael, CA

Distributed by Publishers Group West

Library of Congress Cataloging-in-Publication Data

Lipton, Chet
    Walking easy in the Swiss Alps / Chet & Carolee Lipton :
  [photographs by Chet Lipton, except as noted].
        p.   cm.
    Includes indexes.
    ISBN 0-933469-15-2 : $9.95
      1. Hiking—Switzerland—Alps, Swiss—Guidebooks. 2. Walking-
  -Switzerland—Alps. Swiss—Guidebooks. 3. Alps, Swiss
  (Switzerland)—Guidebooks.   I. Lipton, Carolee. II. Title
    GV199.44.S92A445   1993
    914.94'7—dc20   93-3338
                                                           CIP

10 9 8 7 6 5 4 3 2

To Barbara, Steve and Sue Lipton
The next generation of *Easy Walkers*

Contents

Switzerland
Bern
Interlaken
Lauterbrunnen
Kandersteg
Lake Geneva
Geneva
Saas-Fee
Champex

Zurich

Lucerne

Engelberg

Meiringen

Arosa

Samedan

Pontresina

St. Moritz

BECOMING AN EASY WALKER

It is said that the first pair of shoes proud Swiss parents purchase for their children is most probably a pair of tiny hiking boots. The Swiss love to walk...and the Swiss love walkers. This guidebook was written for *active adults* who enjoy walking, prefer the exhilarating outdoors, and have a need to fulfill a quest for discovery. It is a "how-to book," filled with carefully detailed day-walks, comfortable sightseeing excursions, and personal hints that are beneficial to the more mature walker.

Every activity described in the following chapters has been experienced and edited by the authors to meet the needs of the active adult walker (and perhaps those juniors, under fifty, who think they can keep up). Travelers of all ages walk on the intricate and fascinating network of Swiss hiking trails, and use the incredibly clean and efficient Swiss public transportation system.

Each of the sections in this guide is devoted to a particularly beautiful village or mountain area, and includes a brief description of the location, public transportation, additional activities, excursions to very special nearby points of interest and detailed instructions for each walk. The following towns have been chosen: Saas-Fee, Zermatt and Champex in the Valais, Lauterbrunnen and Kandersteg in the Bernese Oberland and Samedan in the Engadine. These mountain areas were picked because of their local charm, availability of public transportation, reasonably priced but comfortable accommodations, proximity to great walking and exciting excursions.

Suitable walks are described in detail, ranging from short, tranquil lakeside walks to longer, high-level, pine-forested trails, all within the capability and range of most active adults. Each walk and excursion is planned to give *Easy Walkers* maximum visual and physical pleasure.

The "walking time" listed before each walk is *actual* walking time, with little variation for resting, picture-taking, lunch, snacks, sightseeing and transportation. Extra time is left to the discretion of each *Easy Walker*, so that an average day, with a three-hour walk scheduled, usually begins by 9:00 am and ends back in your hotel by 4:00 pm.

Every walk is preceded by a short paragraph describing the location, followed by directions on how to arrive at the start of the walk from the base village. *Unless specifically mentioned, the paths are well-maintained, and the ascents and descents can be accomplished by a recreational walker of any age, in good health.* In many cases, options are provided to modify the walk, if necessary, by using a train or bus.

Each of the activities, excursions and walks in this book can be completed in one day. Some begin with a mountain railway or cable car, while others are gentle walks through the forest or around a lake. Many are above the tree line, across a glacier, or descend through alpine meadows resounding with the harmonious clanging of Swiss cowbells providing an unforgettable accompaniment to *Easy Walking*.

The Swiss alps have over 22,000 miles of "wanderwegs" and "bergwegs," most well-signed and easily followed. The paths you will walk on were chosen for their beauty, walking time and ease of use; but be warned—not all the hikes are "easy." Many will joyously challenge your capabilities with ascents, descents and mixed terrain. However—*Walking Easy* aficionados can handle them. Walking is not just for the young—it is also for the young at heart. It is not uncommon for octogenarians to be slowly but steadily wending their way along their favorite trail. The Swiss have created a wonderful trail system. It is the best way to see the magnificent countryside, and walkers are welcome almost everywhere in their hiking boots and backpacks.

You can do it — just tuck a copy of "Walking Easy" in your pocket and you're on your way!

Timing is Everything

Best Months for an Alpine Walking Experience: The weather can vary within this small country—the Valais is noted for its sunny and dry days, while the Bernese Oberland gets more rain, and the Ticino region is hotter than other areas in summer. Of course, the higher the altitude, the colder it becomes, especially after the sun sets. The tree line is about 6,500 ft., and the snow line in summer can be at 9,000 ft. The real alps, or meadows, used by the Swiss for pasture, are between the tree line and the snow. The word "alp," originally referred to these high pastures, but it now means the entire mountain area.

> ☞ **HINT: Insulated jackets or vests are a necessity if you are spending time in mountain areas even in summer.**

City			Average High Temperatures			
	May	June	July	Aug	Sept	Oct
Zermatt	46	52	58	53	52	38
St. Moritz	50	59	63	61	58	50
Lucerne	65	70	76	77	70	52
Montreux	65	70	77	76	70	56
Zurich	67	74	77	76	68	58
Interlaken	67	72	71	72	68	59
Geneva	67	74	77	76	70	58
Lugano	70	77	81	81	74	61

Deciding the best time of year to walk in the Swiss Alps depends on what you enjoy most in the way of scenery and weather. The alpine flowers begin to bloom in late May and are at their peak from mid-June through July. The colors in the meadows are an artist's palette—red, yellow, white, blue and purple—alpenrose, buttercups, snowbells, gentians and monkshood—contrasting with the green grass of pastureland. July and August are the warmest months and also the most popular tourist months. September offers fewer tourists, lower temperatures, clearer views, less rain in the lower elevations but less snow in higher elevations. The hiking season usually begins in mid-June and ends in mid-October.

> ☞ **HINT: To avoid the crowds, June and September are your best bets.**

In the beginning of June, snow can still cover some of the trails at higher elevations, but the views of the snow-covered peaks contrasting with the riotous colors of the alpine meadow flowers are breathtaking. September weather is usually clearer than other months of the year, with cloudless blue skies the norm, however, the snow has melted from the tops of many of the lower peaks, and the meadow flowers are now dried pods, blowing in the fields. Whichever month you choose, walking on the network of Swiss trails will be exhilarating.

Switzerland by Train, Bus and Boat

The Swiss public transportation system is probably the best in the world. It functions efficiently and smoothly, depending on a complex network linking trains, buses and boats. *Easy Walkers* will find that it may not be necessary to rent a car in Switzerland—the trains, buses and boats are clean and reliable, and have the ability to "leave the driving to us." Our readers can sit back and enjoy the superb views without worrying about hairpin turns or city traffic.

The Swiss National Tourist Office can send you a brochure, "Switzerland by Train, Bus and Boat." This pamphlet acquaints travelers with varied types of transportation discounts. On one side of this brochure is a large map of the Swiss Travel System. This is *not* a road map, only a public transportation map, and *Easy Walkers* are advised to put it in an accessible place for easy reference.

> ☞ **HINT: 2nd class rail travel in Switzerland is just as clean and almost as comfortable as 1st class—we recommend 2nd class savings. Post buses are one class.**

☞ HINT: Train cars are marked with a large "1" or "2" to denote class, and a cigarette with a line drawn through it graphically indicates the non-smoking sections.

☞ HINT: The ever-present yellow PTT (Postal, Telegraph and Telephone Service) buses can carry *Easy Walkers* to remote valleys and across high alpine passes. It's a comfortable and inexpensive way see the Alps.

Boats traverse Switzerland's major lakes and rivers, and they are a slower, more relaxing way to enjoy the scenery. There are old paddle-wheel steamers on the lakes of Brienz, Lucerne, Geneva and Zurich, that date from before World War I.

☞ HINT: "Gëpack" or "baggage system" is an invaluable aid. Bring your luggage to the rail or bus station and pay a small charge. It will be sent to your next destination. Travel easy with only your backpack!

☞ HINT: At all rail stations, large white posters indicate arriving trains ("Ankunft" or "Arrivée"), and yellow posters show departing trains ("Abfahrt" or "Départ"). They are arranged by hour and minute, such as:
ABFAHRT
9:00 am Lucerne
9:01 am Spiez
9:02 am Bern

☞ HINT: Bus stops in small towns post the PTT schedule on a small white card at the bus stop. Since buses may run infrequently in out-of-the-way areas, check the schedule before settling down for lunch or an afternoon snack.

The following are important adjuncts to the railway system, the buses operated by the PTT, and the lake and river boats:

Cable Cars ("luftseilbahnen" or "téléphériques") - large, enclosed cars holding up to 100 people, running on a fixed schedule. A famous cable car system runs from Stechelberg to the Schilthorn. (See Excursion #4 in the Lauterbrunnen section.)

Chairlifts ("sesselbahnen" or "télésièges") - move continuously, and are open to the weather. They are usually single or double-chair systems. We take a chairlift from Beatenburg to the Niederhorn to begin Excursion #14 in the Lauterbrunnen section.

Gondolas ("gondelbahnen" or "télécabines") - hold four to eight people and are enclosed. *Easy Walkers* will use the gondola from Saas-Fee to Hannig to begin Walk #1 in the Saas-Fee section.

Funiculars - mountain railways pulled up and down a steep incline by a cable. The Harder Kulm outside of Interlaken is a good example of this type of mountain railway. Check Excursion #2 in the Lauterbrunnen section.

Cogwheel Railways (rack and pinion railways) - move by a toothed wheel connecting into the matching teeth of the rail. One of the most famous cogwheel railways goes to the Jungfraujoch, through the Eiger and Mönch mountains of the Bernese Oberland. (See Excursion #6 in the Lauterbrunnen section.)

Swiss Discount Travel

Swiss Pass: This is the most convenient of the discount tickets. It entitles users to unlimited travel on the entire public transportation system, including railways, lake steamers, postal buses and to purchase discount tickets on funiculars, cable cars and mountain railways at 25% discount.

Duration	2nd Class	1st Class
3 out of 15 days	$148	$222
8 days	$186	$266
15 days	$214	$312
1 month	$296	$430
(As of 1993)		

Swiss Card: This discount card entitles the purchaser to one free round trip, plus half fare for all additional trips. From your entry point into Switzerland—whether by air or at any border station—your destination city or town within the country (no matter how many changes of train, bus, etc.) is free, and you receive a free trip back from the same or another place, to any departure point. You may purchase an unlimited number of tickets at half-price on all scheduled transportation, plus 25% to 50% discount on most mountain transportation.

	2nd Class	**1st Class**
1 month (As of 1993)	$96	$118

☞ **HINT: If you are planning an 8 to 30 day *Easy Walking* trip, we recommend buying a Swiss Pass. You won't have to stand in line to buy a ticket—just board your train, bus or boat and show the conductor your Pass. We have used both the Swiss Pass and the Swiss Card, and found that the end cost is about the same, but the Pass is more convenient. With the Pass, the cost is paid before you leave, and traveling is ticket-free. With the Card the initial cost is less expensive, but then you must buy a 1/2 price ticket each time you use public transportation. Swiss Cards and Swiss Passes are available through travel agents.**

Comfortable Inns and Hotels

Accommodations in Switzerland range from five-star, world-class, deluxe hotels, to campgrounds with tents, and "matratzenlager"—dormitories in mountain hotels. The quality of a hotel (and its prices), can be judged by the number of stars awarded to it: five stars denotes deluxe; four stars, first class; three stars, superior; two stars, standard; and one star, minimum. For our readers we recommend three star hotels for comfort, quality of food, and price. If you prefer to eat dinner at different restaurants—usually more expensive than dinner at your hotel on half-board—try a hotel "garni," a hotel that serves breakfast only, and is rated on the same star system as full hotels.

Furnished chalets and rental apartments are a viable alternative to hotels, and a list of agencies handling these rentals is available from the Swiss National Tourist Office. The local tourist office in each town in Switzerland can also provide lists of places to rent. Write to them and contact the home or apartment owners by mail.

"E + G Hotels" is the Swiss concept of "bed and breakfast." The initials stand for "einfach" and "gemütlich," German for simple and cozy. These 220 guesthouses are located throughout Switzerland. A brochure listing their addresses and telephone numbers is available from the Swiss National Tourist Office.

The official "Swiss Hotel Guide" is updated yearly. It lists all members of the Swiss Hotel Association—about 80% of the country's hotels—and gives full details on each hotel—from the number of beds, and the cost of the room, to whether credit cards are accepted and pets are allowed. Write to the Swiss National Tourist Office for this free guide.

Winter is the more expensive tourist season in ski resorts such as Zermatt, Saas-Fee and St. Moritz. Ski towns have built hotels and apartments to handle the winter crowds. They are not always filled for the spring, summer and autumn seasons, so rates are lower and rooms may be easier to obtain.

☞ **HINT: Some of the smaller hotels do not accept credit cards. Use the Hotel Guide to check the end of each listing and note whether the initials AE, MC or V are in the credit card section. If you cannot, or do not wish to pay by credit card, make sure you have bought enough travelers checks to cover your hotel bill, as they do not accept personal checks.**

☞ **HINT: Prices listed for hotels usually include all taxes and tips and full buffet breakfast. Many small hotels do not require a deposit. If you write to them directly, they will confirm the cost of your room and food, and dates of arrival and departure, with a welcoming letter.**

Most of the small hotels in the areas we mention in this book are family-owned and operated. Whatever type you choose, remember that Swiss hotel keepers have the highest standards of service and cleanliness.

Check the Accommodations section of this book for three-star, comfortable, chalet-type hotel recommendations.

Enjoying Swiss Cuisine

Swiss cooking has been influenced by her neighbors— Austria, Germany, France and Italy—and local specialities were developed in valleys isolated by high mountains. *Easy Walkers* should try to sample the local fare.

Cheese - Dairy farming has been part of the Swiss heritage for 2,000 years, and cheese-making is a natural offshoot. Emmentaler and Gruyère are probably the most famous of the more than 100 different varieties of cheese that are produced in hundreds of small dairies in alpine pastures.

Taste any local cheese and enjoy the marvelous, fresh flavor, so unlike the packaged and processed cheeses we've become used to.

Bread - The Swiss choose from over 200 different types of bread. Each canton makes different varieties of breads, and local bakers devise their own specialties. "Vollkornbrot" is a whole grain bread, "Walliser brot" is a dark, heavy bread, and "Halbweiss"—one of the most popular types of bread is like our unseeded rye.

☞ **HINT: "Bitte noch etwas brot," told to your waiter, will bring more of whatever delicious bread is being served.**

Pastries - The Swiss excel in their pastry making—sold in "konditorei" or "patisseries"—pastry shops and tea rooms. Crisp, light meringues filled with whipped cream are a specialty in the Emmental. "Rüeblitorte" is a fluffy, carrot sponge cake from Aargau. "Basler leckerli" are Basel's honey and almond cookies, "biber" is the spiced, honey nut cake of Appenzell, and "tuorta de nusch Engiadinaisa" is a rich walnut pie from the Engadine.

Wine - Swiss wines, grown on many hillsides throughout the country, taste best when they are of recent vintage.

☞ **HINT: In French-speaking Switzerland try the fruity white Fendant and Johannisberg. Dôle is the most popular red wine. In the German-speaking sections, *Easy Walkers* can sample a dry light red wine such as Stammheimer or Klevner, and in the Italian Ticino, try a fruity red Merlot, or Mezzana and Nostrano— stronger dessert wines.**

Beer - Most cities in Switzerland brew excellent varieties of beer.

☞ **HINT: "Ein bier, bitte," is the order for "one beer, please;" while "Ein bier von Interlaken, bitte," is asking for a beer of the Interlaken area.**

Liqueur - The most popular Swiss liqueurs are kirsch—the national drink made from cherry pit juice, pflümli—made from plums, and Williamine—from pears.

☞ **HINT: Prices of bourbon, scotch, etc. are very expensive in Switzerland. Order a local beer, wine or liqueur.**

Mineral Water - Each area of Switzerland produces mineral water—with or without "gas."

> ☞ **HINT: When dining in your hotel, order a large bottle of mineral water and/or wine. At the end of the meal the unused balance is usually recapped and brought to your table the next evening.**

Regional Food Specialities:

Cheese Fondue - Grated Emmantaler and Gruyère, the basis of fondue, are melted in a pot rubbed with garlic, together with white wine, lemon juice, pepper, nutmeg, paprika and kirsch, to form the national dish of Switzerland. Diners sit around a hot, simmering, earthenware pot and use long forks to dip pieces of crusty bread into the hot mixture.

> ☞ **HINT: One should not order water, beer or coffee with fondue—white wine is the traditional beverage.**

Raclette - This word is derived from the French "racler"—to scrape off, and is a speciality in the Valais or French-speaking region of Switzerland. A half wheel of raclette cheese is melted and as the cheese softens, it is scraped onto a plate. Traditional accompaniments to raclette are country bread, small potatoes boiled in their skins, and pickled onions.

> ☞ **HINT: Don't wait for everyone at the table to be served—the flavor of the melted cheese is best when eaten hot.**

At the breakfast buffet, next to the ubiquitous cornflakes, is *müesli*, a national breakfast dish made of an apple grated into cereal containing grains, milk, berries and nuts. Having lunch at a country inn? Try their *gülaschsuppe*, a hearty soup filled with vegetables and meat. Along with fresh, crusty bread, this is a delicious and filling lunch on the trail. Or, sample the *bratwurst*, sausage usually served with grilled onions and *rösti*, potatoes that have been fried and then baked—the national dish of German-speaking Switzerland. If you are vacationing in the Grisons, *bundnerfleisch*, thinly sliced, air-dried beef is a delicacy, and with it all, don't forget a *gemischter salat,* mixed salad. Your dinner might include such specialities as *spätzli and knöpfli*, everyone's favorite dumplings; *kohlrouladen*, stuffed cabbage; or *jagerschnitzel*, pcrk with mushrooms. In Bern, try the *Berner platte*, consisting of boiled beef, ham, sausages, and bacon with sauerkraut, string beans and potatoes—but make sure you are really hungry before tackling this platter! In Zurich you might try *geschnetzeltes kalbfleisch,* sliced veal in cream sauce. And don't forget any of the local fish caught in the clear, cold alpine lakes. Sample the local cuisine—it's tasty, it's fun, and it will complete your *Walking Easy* experience.

Where to Eat and Drink

Hotel Food - Three-star Swiss hotels offer a full buffet breakfast and a four or five course meal for dinner, if you take a room with demi-pension (half board). Hotel food in Switzerland is uniformly excellent, and *Easy Walkers* can take advantage of lower costs by booking with dinner. Buffet breakfast or "frühstück" is included in the room charge and consists of freshly baked bread and rolls (croissants in the French-speaking areas), butter and margarine, jam, sliced cheese, cornflakes, müesli and whole milk (skim or 2% milk is not usually served in Switzerland). Larger buffets may also include sliced cold meats, yoghurts and fresh fruit. Coffee, tea or hot chocolate are included with breakfast but cost extra at dinner.

> ☞ **HINT: Most diners prefer to take their after-dinner coffee later at an outdoor café.**

Dinner can consist of soup or appetizer, salad or salad bar, main meat or fish course with fresh vegetables and potatoes, and dessert.

> ☞ **HINT: Fresh fruit can usually be substituted for the sweet dessert, if desired.**

Restaurant Food - If you decide to eat in a restaurant outside your hotel, notify the hotel desk 24 hours in advance so the day's demi-pension charge can be deducted from your bill.

☞ **HINT: Most restaurants post a special of the day ("tagesteller" or "plat du jour"), which represents the best value on the menu, and is usually three courses.**

☞ **HINT: A 15% service charge is *always* included in your bill. A few small coins may be left on the table if you were pleased with the service.**

☞ **HINT: The Swiss National Tourist Office publishes a list of restaurants serving kosher food in Switzerland.**

When going out for a day of walking, we recommend taking a picnic lunch in your backpack. Buy fresh bread or rolls at the bakery, and select a local cheese and/or sliced cooked meat. Fresh fruit completes a delicious and inexpensive meal. Mustard can be bought in reusable squeeze tubes. Bottled water, juice or soda is available in plastic bottles or cans.

Dressing for the Trail—
From Boots to Backpack

Walking Easy clothing should ideally be both lightweight and layerable. All clothing is not suitable for all types of walking—climate, altitude and time of day during the alpine hiking season are points to consider. *Easy Walkers* must make a decision each day, taking the above factors into consideration.

Shoes and Socks - The most important item for a successful *Walking Easy* experience is a good pair of broken-in, lightweight hiking boots, waterproof if possible. These can be above or below the ankle, with the higher ones providing more support on rocky or steep trails. Do not wear sneakers or sneakers that look like walking boots, as they do not provide the foot support and traction needed. When purchasing good quality lightweight hiking boots, wear the combination of socks that you will use for walking. Experts tell us that socks worn closest to your skin, should *not* be made of cotton. Cotton absorbs perspiration and holds it, possibly producing friction leading to blisters. A lightweight under-sock made of a "hydrophobic" or water-hating synthetic will wick sweat away from your feet and keep them drier. Whether you prefer to wear one or two pair of socks, when purchasing hiking boots, make sure to take into consideration the type of socks you will be wearing on the trail.

> ☞ **HINT: Eliminate your heaviest packable item by wearing your hiking boots on the plane and whenever you travel.**

Outer Clothing - An insulated jacket or vest is essential at higher elevations, and for sightseeing over 10,000 feet, i.e. the Jungfraujoch in the Bernese Oberland and the Klein Matterhorn in Zermatt.

These jackets are easily put into backpacks when not needed on the trail, and can be carried on to the plane.

Rain protection is best provided by a waterproof poncho with a snap-down back to fit over a backpack, or waterproof long pants and jacket. Don't let a drizzle or light rain cancel your walking plans.

> ☞ **HINT: Rain gear should always stay folded at the bottom of your backpack till needed.**

Hats - A hat with a brim provides protection from sun as well as rain.

Pants - Many alpine walkers wear blue jeans—a good choice if they are not skin-tight and do not restrict movement. Cotton chinos are also satisfactory, and in summer, walking shorts of denim and/or chino should be considered. Our favorite walking apparel in any type of climate however, is alpine hiking knickers, fastened below the knee and worn with high socks which protect the legs from bushes and brambles and cold temperatures, but can be rolled down in warmer weather. These knickers, for both men and women, are comfortable for all types of walking, and you'll see them on trails throughout Europe. They can be bought in most sporting goods stores in every town in Switzerland.

Sweaters - Medium-weight sweaters are essential for cool evenings in the mountains, even in summer.

Sweat Shirts - Medium-weight sweat shirts can be layered over short or long-sleeved cotton knits for hiking.

Shirts - While many people prefer 100% natural fibers for comfort, a cotton-polyester blend in a knit or regular shirt can be used for ease of laundering—a cotton-poly blend will usually dry overnight. Short-sleeved knits, along with a few turtleneck long-sleeved shirts, are essential for layering under sweaters or sweat shirts, both day and evening.

Back Pack - Each *Easy Walker* should carry a lightweight, nylon backpack with wide, extra-heavy, foam, adjustable shoulder straps. Three to four roomy, outside zipper compartments are necessary to organize backpacking essentials, i.e., camera equipment, lunch, water, sunscreen, binoculars, emergency roll of toilet tissue, raingear, jacket or sweater, etc.

Fanny Pack - Use a well-made, comfortable waist pack to carry money, travelers checks, passport, etc. No pocketbook or purse is necessary on a walking vacation. Leave your hands free for your walking stick and camera.

Walking Stick - We recommend a walking cane or stick with a pointed tip for all *Easy Walkers*. These sticks are an indispensable aid to balance when walking downhill or on rocky terrain. They come in many sizes and styles and can usually be bought at your first arrival destination in Switzerland.

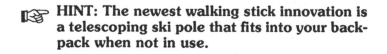 **HINT: The newest walking stick innovation is a telescoping ski pole that fits into your backpack when not in use.**

Luggage Carrier - A small, fold-up luggage carrier is necessary to transport your luggage from the train or bus station to the hotel, if hotel transportation is not available.

Pack Light and Right for a Two-Week Walking Vacation

Keep your luggage small, lightweight and expandable, even when using a luggage carrier.

1. Wear your hiking boots for all traveling—they can be heavy and bulky to carry. Take them off on the plane and change to a pair of scuffs you have put into your backpack.

2. On the plane, wear comfortable slacks or jeans, knit shirt and an unlined jacket, along with your fanny pack. A lightweight warm-up suit can be a good alternative—the jacket can be worn when it is too warm for an insulated jacket.

3. Every *Easy Walker* should have a lightweight backpack used as carry-on luggage. When traveling, your backpack should include:

   a) all drugs and toiletries, with prescriptions in a separate zippered pouch for easy accessibility.

   b) for the plane—one change of socks, underwear and knit shirt, rolled into a plastic bag.

   c) scuff slippers for plane and bedroom use.

   d) lightweight insulated jacket (carry this if not packable)

   e) waterproof outerwear

   f) reading material for the plane

   g) roll of toilet paper in a plastic bag

   h) incidentals such as: binoculars, compass, whistle, tiny flashlight, pocketknife, plastic bags, sewing kit, sunglasses, small travel clock, address book or preprinted labels, small packs of tissues and "handiwipes," *Walking Easy* guidebook.

   i) photographic equipment unless carried separately.

Easy Walkers' Unisex Packing Checklist

✔ **Amount Item**

__ 6	underwear
__ 3	bras
__ 7 pr.	socks (3 hiking, 2 "undersocks," 2 evening)
__ 2 pr.	shoes (1 hiking, 1 casual)
__ 1 pr.	scuffs
__ 1	belt
__ 1	pajamas/nightgown
__ 1	robe (optional)
__ 1	bathing suit (optional)
__ 2	sweaters
__ 1	sweat shirt
__ 1	jacket, insulated
__ 1	jacket, lightweight
__ 2	hiking pants or knickers
__ 2	casual slacks
__ 2	shirts, blouses, long-sleeved
__ 1	walking shorts
__ 4	knit shirts, short-sleeved
__ 2	knit shirts, long-sleeeved, turtleneck
__ 1	hat
__ 1	rain gear

☞ HINT: It is not necessary to bring a dress, skirt, sport jacket, stockings, dress shoes or pocketbook on this walking vacation. However, a classic mix of slacks layered with shirts and sweaters is essential and can take you to dinner or sightseeing. In fact, the mix and match combination of 2 pair of slacks, 2 knit turtlenecks, 2 long-sleeved cotton shirts, and 2 sweaters, creates inumerable combinations and has taken the authors through 2 months of alpine evenings!

☞ HINT: Small towns may *not* have laundry facilities or hotel valet service, and if you wash underwear, socks, and knit shirts every night before dinner, you'll always be ahead. Remember: clothes can take two days to dry if they are 100% cotton. Shirts or underwear that contain poly-cotton will dry overnight.

☞ HINT: On your first day in Switzerland, buy "Express," a pack of ten individual detergents. You can leave any leftovers and it eliminates the need of carrying it from home.

For Your Information— From Telephones to Tipping

Credit Cards - Most stores and hotels accept credit cards, but some smaller hotels and mountain inns do not. Take enough travelers checks to cover your stay.

☞ HINT: Charging can work in your favor, but if the dollar declines by the time your bill arrives, you will be paying a bit more.

Customs - Residents of non-European countries such as the United States may bring into Switzerland: 400 cigarettes, one quart of alcoholic beverage in excess of 15 proof and two quarts below 15 proof—age 18 and older. There are no restrictions on the import or export of any currency.

Returning from Switzerland to the United States, American citizens may bring back $400 in duty-free items if they've been outside the United States for at least 48 hours and not claimed exemptions in the previous thirty days. A flat rate of 10% is assessed for items valued at over $400. You may bring in antiques over 100 years old duty-free, with proof of authenticity. Gifts up to a total of $50 per day can be mailed home without declaring them on your customs form.

☞ HINT: Keep all receipts of purchases in one place where they can be easily retrieved.

Documents - A valid passport is necessary for every traveler entering Switzerland.

> **HINT: Before leaving the country, photocopy the information on your passport pages in case it is lost. Since you'll be carrying the original passport in your "fanny pack," put the copy in another location.**

Electricity - Electricity is 220 volt, 50 cycle, AC. Bring a transformer and adaptor plug with you for shavers, hair dryers, etc.

Gifts - Handmade products of Switzerland are usually high in quality. In large cities such as Zürich and Bern, look for shops specializing in Swiss crafts. Local department stores are also good places to shop. Gift items to bring back can include: clocks and watches, Swiss army knives, handkerchiefs, embroidery, wood carvings, music boxes and chocolate.

Government -Modern Switzerland is a confederation of more than 3,000 communes. Years ago, neighboring communes formed 23 cantons, with their own constitutions, laws and governments, leaving only foreign policy, national defense, economic policy, etc. to the Federal Parliament.

The legislative body of Switzerland consists of a National Council, elected on the basis of proportional representation, and a 46-member Council of States, where every canton has two representatives. The executive body, or Federal Council, is made up of seven members, elected for four years, responsible for heading different departments. The president of the Council serves a one-year term and leads the Confederation.

Insurance - There are three types of insurance for travelers - contact your travel agent for companies offering such policies.
   1. health and accident
   2. trip cancellation
   3. missing luggage

Before purchasing additional travel insurance, *Easy Walkers* should review their existing policies and determine whether coverage is adequate for overseas travel.

☞ **HINT: Medicare only covers United States travelers to Mexico and Canada. Check your Medicare supplement for overseas coverage.**

"Homeowner" policies may cover luggage, theft and/or plane tickets. Call your insurance agent.

Language - The four official languages of Switzerland are German, spoken by 65% of the population; French, 18%; Italian, 12%; and Romansch, spoken by only 1% of the people in the southeastern mountains. However, the German of the native Swiss is called "Schwyzer Deutsch," a dialect different in vocabulary, pronunciation and grammar from classical German, the language used for speeches, teaching, literature, business, and radio or TV. French and Italian are the same as that spoken in their native countries, although rural and mountain villages in some areas have developed local variations. Romansch can be heard in the Engadine. English is usually spoken in even the smallest village.

Medications - If you are taking a prescription drug, bring more than just an adequate supply, plus a prescription for the drug using its generic name, in case it is neccesary for a local doctor to write a new prescription. Also, carry over-the-counter medications to counteract diarrhea, sunburn, constipation, indigestion, cuts and bruises, colds and allergies, etc. Put together a small first aid kit to carry in your backpack while walking—band-aids, antibiotic cream, aspirin, allergy pills—and of course, an effective sunscreen.

☞ **HINT: When traveling, always carry your medications in your backpack in case there is a problem with checked luggage.**

☞ **HINT: If you wear glasses, carry a spare pair, and a copy of your prescription.**

Money - The basic unit of currency in Switzerland is the Swiss Franc (SF), composed of 100 centimes. Paper bank notes are in 10, 20, 50, 100, 500 and 1,000 SF denominations, while coins are 5, 10, 20 and 50 centimes, and 1, 2 and 5 franc pieces.

The exchange rate fluctuates constantly, but to convert Swiss francs to U.S. dollars, multiply the number of francs by the exchange rate. For example, if your hotel room is 150 SF per day and the exchange rate is 1 SF = .70, multiply 150 by .70—your hotel room will cost $105.

 HINT: Before leaving home, buy travelers checks and carry no more than $200 in cash. You can purchase American travelers checks such as American Express, Citicorp, etc., but when you convert them to Swiss francs you'll usually pay a commission. To avoid the service charge and the waiting lines, purchase travelers checks in 100 Swiss franc denominations. Most large banks and AAA offer this service to their customers. These are easily converted to cash or used as cash with no extra charge.

HINT: Money can be changed at all airports and railroad stations, as well as banks. Look for windows marked, "Geldwechsel," "Cambio" and "Change."

Newspapers - Swiss newspapers are published in German, French and Italian, but even in small towns, a store can usually be found that sells the *International Herald Tribune*, published in English Monday through Saturday. Newsstands, or "kiosks" are also found at railroad stations.

Physicians - If you need a doctor while vacationing in Switzerland, the hotel owner can put you in touch with one. If you are in a small town, be prepared to travel to a larger town or city for specialized care. When you see a doctor, the fee is paid after the consultation.

☞ **HINT: Make sure you receive a bill marked "paid," and contact your own health insurance for reimbursement when you return home.**

Post Office - Letter boxes in Switzerland are painted bright yellow. Every small town has a post office, usually opening at 7:30 am and closing at 6:30 pm, with a noon to 2:00 pm lunch break. Saturday closing is 12 noon. Mail from home can be forwarded to a Swiss post office for collection. Envelopes must have: a return name and address, name of the person who will collect the mail, the words "Poste Restante," plus the name of the town preceded by the ZIP or post code. For example:

Mr. Alan Bell

Poste Restante

CH-7050 Arosa, Switzerland

If not picked up within thirty days, this mail will be returned to sender. A passport is necessary identification to pick up these letters.

Restrooms - Swiss lavatories are generally clean and modern, and most are free in public places, but if you find a coin is necessary, it will usually be a 20 centime piece. The area of Switzerland you are traveling in will prescribe the names on public restroom doors, known in general as "WC": women - "damen," "frauen," "signore," "femmes," "dames;" men - "herren," "signori," "hommes," "messieurs."

Senior Discounts - If you are a women over 62 or a man over 65, "Season for Seniors," listing hotels offering senior discounts, is available from the Swiss National Tourist Office. If you reserve a room at any of these listed accommodations, indicate that you would like the senior rate.

Shopping Hours - Stores in Switzerland are usually open Monday to Friday, 8:00 am to 12:15 pm and 1:30 pm to 6:30 pm. Saturday the stores are either open in the morning or afternoon, except in tourist towns such as Grindelwald, where they may be open all day in season. Stores are closed on Sunday. Check in each area for exact opening and closing times.

Telephone - Some helpful telephone numbers to carry with you:

Directory assistance - 111
Tourist information - 120
Police emergency - 117
Ambulance - 144
Fire - 118
Weather forecast - 162

To use a coin operated telephone:

1. Lift the receiver and insert 1 SF coin.
2. A dial tone will begin.
3. Insert coins for each message unit, up to 5 SF.
4. To call locally, dial the number after you hear the dial tone.
5. For other places in Switzerland, dial the city code, then the telephone number.
6. To telephone a foreign country, dial the country's code number, then the area code, then the telephone number.

☞ **HINT: Use public phone booths instead of hotel phones because of high service charges that can be added to your bill.**

Time - Swiss time is six hours ahead of Eastern Standard Time in the United States. Switzerland uses European time, based on the 24-hour clock, and all timetables are written in this manner. Know that 13:10 pm is 1:10 pm in the United States, and 18:40 pm is 6:40 pm.

Tipping - Restaurant bills have a 15% service charge added to the cost. It is customary, however, to leave some small coins on the table if you enjoyed the service.

Tourist Information Offices -These offices, designated in Switzerland by a large "i", are a valuable friend to the hiker. You'll usually find them on the main street in even the smallest communities, near or in the railroad station in larger towns. The personnel are multilingual and friendly, and can help with everything from hotel reservations to local hiking maps. When preparing for your trip, write to the travel bureau in the towns you intend visiting, and ask them to send you information on hotels, walking and sightseeing activities.

☞ **HINT: Send all overseas requests by airmail for faster delivery.**

The Swiss National Tourist Office (SNTO) can provide information on accommodations, maps, rail/bus/boat timetables, sightseeing and general information about every aspect of a vacation in Switzerland. If you live in the area, stop in to see them and talk to their courteous and helpful staff. Or, write to the Swiss National Tourist Office at:

608 Fifth Ave., New York, NY 10020. (212)757-5944
150 N. Michigan Ave., Chicago, IL 60601. (312)630-5840
222 N. Sepulveda Blvd., El Segundo, CA 90245. (213)335-5980
260 Stockton St., San Francisco, CA 94108. (415)362-2260

United States Embassy and Consulates:
Embassy:
Jubilaumsstrasse 93, Bern. Tel. 031/43-70-11
Consulates:
1-3 avenue de la Paix, Geneva. Tel. 022/733-55-37
Zollikerstrasse 141, Zurich. Tel. 011/55-25-66

Water - Considered safe to drink in Switzerland, but many visitors use bottled water for drinking purposes.

Rules Of The Road

- Paths in Switzerland are usually well-signed and marked. The signposts list time, rather than distance. "1 std." indicates "1 hour" "Std." is the abbreviation for the German "stunde," or "hour." *Easy Walkers* should allow at least 25% more time than the signpost estimates.
- Yellow signs represent "wanderwegs" or "chemin pedestres," lower-level paths through easy hills and lower mountain slopes. White-red-white signs denote higher level "bergwegs" or "chemin de montagnes," mountain trails through more difficult terrain. These colors may also be marked on rocks or trees to continue the path.

- Plan the route by checking this book and local hiking maps, before you begin the walk.
- Ask about local weather conditions at your hotel, and adjust the day's activities accordingly.
- Always tell someone about your planned route, either a friend or someone at the hotel.
- Take your time, especially at higher altitudes—alpine walking is not a race. Walking at a slow, steady pace provides time for enjoyment of the trail and the scenery.
- Never leave the marked trail.
- Turning back is not a disgrace—if you feel the trail is too difficult, return on the same path or check public transportation in the area.
- In case of an accident, stay calm and send for help. If this is not possible, use the standard alpine distress signal with your whistle or flashlight: 6 signals, spaced evenly within 1 minute, pause for 1 minute, then repeat.
- Many wildflowers are protected by law. Appreciate their beauty, but don't pick them—leave them for others to enjoy.
- Don't litter. Take out what you bring in. Carry plastic bags in your backpack for this purpose.
- Close any gate you've opened—you don't want to be responsible for the livestock straying.

The major purpose of any walking trip is to have fun.
So . . . take a hike . . . you can do it!

Explanation of Symbols

All walks can be accomplished by a recreational walker of any age, in good health. The following *Walking Easy* symbols are displayed at the beginning of each walk.

Gentle, lower-level walks with few ascents and descents, through valleys and around lakes.

Comfortable ascents and descents over mixed terrain.

More challenging ascents and descents on parts of the trail.

Trail Maps: Maps are visual indications of the walking route and are *not* drawn to scale.

SAAS-FEE

Saas-Fee, a picturesque, traffic-free village of 1,000 residents, ensconced high on a glacial plateau at 5,873 ft., has evolved over the years from a modest agricultural hamlet to a fashionable, all-season resort in the southern Valais region of Switzerland. Visitors are immediately overwhelmed by the all-encompassing beauty of its surrounding mountains and glaciers. The southern end of this alpine village flows into serene pasture, ending abruptly as mountains and glaciers rise almost vertically and appear to encircle and swallow tiny Saas-Fee. This "Pearl of the Alps" sits beneath a giant, frozen wave of ice and snow—whose awesome magnificence permeates every nook and cranny of the village.

The Zermatt and Saas valleys in south-central Switzerland's Valais region are divided only by the Mischabel mountain range. However, Saas-Fee remains virtually unknown, while Zermatt evolved into a highly visible tourist center for visitors from around the world. This small, charming resort attracts walkers of all ages—and of course, *Easy Walkers* anxious to sample the enticing paths of the Saas-Fee hiking areas. Many clearly marked trails invite you through woods filled with the aroma of pine needles, into gorges surging with cascading water, and over rocks and ridges with breathtaking panoramas.

Saas-Fee is ringed by more than twelve mountains over 13,000 ft. including the Dom at 14,941 ft., the highest mountain entirely in Switzerland, and in the distance, the imposing Monte Rosa at 15,204 ft., the tallest mountain in Switzerland, but with its south face in Italy. A long narrow valley lies below Saas-Fee, offering remarkable hiking options. Saas-Almagell, in this valley at 5,450 ft., is the gateway to the Monte Moro Pass into Italy on the far side of the Mattmark Reservoir. Walkers can hike the length of the valley, from Saas Almagell

to Saas-Balen, on well-marked trails that pass through centuries-old alpine hamlets, crossing streams and winding through
enchanting pine forests, never very far away from PTT bus
stops, for a return to Saas-Fee.

Imposing glaciers offer unforgettable hiking options. The
glacier walk from the Felskinn cable car station at 9,850 ft., to
the Britanniahütte, staffed by the Swiss Alpine Club, is
reasonably level, somewhat demanding, and particularly
rewarding. Other walks feature families of marmots at the Spielboden cable stop, magnificent views of Saas-Fee from Hannig
at 7,710 ft., and an incredible close-up of the Fee glacier, seen
as you descend the mountain from Spielboden to Saas-Fee,
where most hikers converge for an afternoon snack at a favorite
cafe or tea room.

The sheltered location of Saas-Fee has taught the residents
to be concerned for each other, and each other's livestock as
well. Small gardens are planted everywhere, and the greens
from freshly picked vegetables are saved in boxes for livestock
feed. Stale bread is not thrown away, but delivered daily to
public lockers marked "Hart Brot," to use for the animals. The
people of Saas-Fee have learned to be self-sufficient, caring and
conservative, and it is not unusual to still see local women in
traditional peasant dress, shopping and walking in the narrow,
old streets.

Saas-Fee is dotted with centuries old feed barns called
mazots, cornered on four to six round, flat, chiseled stones that
serve as elevated foundations, so feed for livestock can be stored
during frigid winter months. The round stones prevent rodents
from climbing into the mazots and destroying the feed. These
marvelous landmark buildings serve as a reminder of earlier
days, as they proudly stand along the streets and meadows of
Saas-Fee.

Modern-day Saas-Fee has evolved from an ancient mule
path to paved walking and shopping streets which traverse this
typical alpine village. Hotels are expanding and modernizing to
cater to skiers, hikers and climbers. Food preparation is inspired
by French cuisine of the Valais region. Cream sauces are used
extensively for entrees, vegetables and of course, desserts. *Easy*

Walkers may find this rich "French style" a bit disconcerting—you might try to ask for "sauce on the side,"—if you dare.

Saas-Fee offers hikers 170 miles of well-signed trails, and opportunities for excursions down into the valley, as well as on mountains and glaciers. "The Pearl of the Alps" provides the atmosphere of a typical Swiss mountain village, while catering to the special needs of all types of visitors—those who have arrived to take part in the more strenuous activities of hiking and mountain climbing, and others content to enjoy the awesome panorama surrounding the resort from sun-terraces on the heights, or from their balconies outside comfortable Saas-Fee hotels.

Transportation

Geneva Airport to Saas-Fee - The Geneva Airport is modern and spacious. While waiting for luggage to arrive, use the money exchange in the customs inspection area to buy Swiss francs. After clearing customs, note the large signs marked "Gare," emblazoned with a symbol of a train. Follow these signs into the connecting railroad station and validate your Swiss Card or Swiss Pass at any ticket window. Take one of the frequent trains to "Geneva Central," and change for the train to Brig, stopping at Montreux and Martigny. Remember to look for the railway cars clearly marked with a non-smoking symbol and a "2" for second class, if that's your preference.

A seat on the right side facing forward will present a good view of Lake Geneva and its charming, old towns. On your left, away from the lake, are rolling hills covered with vineyards. After stops in Lausanne, Vevey, Montreux and Martigny, the train heads east towards Brig, with snow-capped mountains visible in the distance.

In Brig, change for the PTT bus—the only form of public transportation into Saas-Fee. This bus stops at several busy little towns, taking on and discharging local passengers. After leaving Saas-Grund, the bus begins to climb, stopping only at a few mountain hamlets and to let off local school children. After a few miles of hairpin, scenic turns, you will enter the traffic-free village of Saas-Fee. There are large car-parks for visitors' and local residents' autos. Bus reservations are necessary on busy weekends and summer days, so call ahead from the Geneva Airport at 028 23 66 57. A reminder to *Easy Walkers*: when leaving Saas-Fee, make return reservations at the bus station in town at least 24 hours in advance.

If you are traveling to Saas-Fee from a town in Switzerland or Europe other than Geneva, remember to change for the bus in Brig, Visp or Stalden. Check timetables for best connections.

Sample Timetable:

Geneva Airport to Geneva	**Take any train**
Geneva to Brig	**11:48 am dep.**
Brig	**14:11 pm arr. (2:11 pm)**
Brig to Saas-Fee (PTT Bus)	**14:15 pm dep. (2:15 pm)**
Saas-Fee	**15:20 pm arr. (3:20 pm)**

Activities in Saas-Fee

Here are some activities available in Saas-Fee on days when additions or alternatives to walking are desired. The Saas-Fee Tourist Bureau is across from the PTT bus terminal.

Ask for a guest card from your hotel immediately after arrival. This entitles you to local discounts.

- Tennis - 7 outdoor courts are at the Kalbermatten Sports Centre and 2 indoor courts are in the Bielen Recreation Centre. Call 031 51 66 131 for information.
- Badminton - indoors at Bielen Recreation Centre.
- Swimming - indoor pool at Bielen Recreation Centre.
- Sauna and Solarium - at Bielen Recreation Centre.
- Ping Pong and Billiards - at Bielen Recreation Centre.
- Mini-golf
- Saaser Museum - a variety of exhibits are displayed about local culture and customs, mineralogy and glacialogy. The museum is located in the center of town near the church.

Saas-Fee offers a wide range of cultural events in the summer months. These include yodelling and folklore festivals, and concerts.

Excursions in and Around Saas-Fee

This section introduces day excursions that *Easy Walkers* will enjoy when an alternative to walking is desired. Be sure to check local timetables for best connections if public transportation is being used. Bus reservations may be needed from Saas-Fee to Stalden or Brig, and return. They can be made at the PTT station in Saas-Fee.

1. Spielboden-Längfluh (Saas-Fee) - The gondola/cable car to Spielboden and Längfluh is in two sections, about a 20-minute walk from the center of town, past the soccer fields and tennis courts.

A. Saas-Fee to Spielboden - This station of the Längfluh cable car at over 8,000 ft., offers close-up views of the Fee glacier and Spielboden's colonies of tame marmots, who love to be fed. (See #2 in Walks section)

B. Spielboden to Längfluh - The top station at 9,400 ft., brings *Easy Walkers* to the very edge of the Fee glacier. There are spectacular views of this glacier and the village of Saas-Fee, surrounded by its snow-covered mountains. On a clear day, you can see summer skiers on the Mittelallalin slopes. There are restaurants with facilities at both Spielboden and Längfluh.

2. Felskinn - Mittelallalin (Saas-Fee) - The Felskinn-Mittelallalin ride is a 2-stage gondola/subway, reached by walking up the main street, past the church. The lift station is clearly marked and is a 20-minute walk from the center of town.

A. Saas-Fee to Felskinn - This station affords a fascinating view of the massive circle of peaks and glaciers surrounding Saas-Fee. (See Walk #3.)

B. Felskinn to Mittelallalin - The second section to Mittelallalin at 11,482 ft., is the world's highest underground railway—Metro-Alpin—transporting visitors to the world's highest revolving restaurant and sun deck, where sitting and watching the vast, snowy, glacial spectacle can become hypnotic. *Easy Walkers*, remember to use that sunscreen.

3. Hannig (Saas-Fee) - The lift station to Hannig can be found by following the signs on the main street directing you up above the town. The four-person cable cars run continuously and bring riders to yet another panoramic viewpoint. Many walks begin from this point, but today you can just relax and enjoy the large sun-terrace adjacent to the cafeteria. (See Walk #1.)

4. Plattjen (Saas-Fee) - Gondolas lift you to over 8,500 ft. from Saas-Fee to Plattjen. A splendid panorama of the mountains, glaciers and the village of Saas-Fee, can be found at the top. (See Walk #2.)

5. Kreuzboden (Saas-Grund) - This gondola in Saas-Grund rises to 7,200 ft. and provides another perspective of the Mischabel range of mountains, across the valley in Saas-Fee. (See Walk #5.)

Directions to Saas-Grund and Kreuzboden: Take the bus at the PTT station in Saas-Fee for the short ride to Saas-Grund, the first stop. Follow the signs in town to the lift station. They are emblazoned with a picture of a cable car. A 15-minute ride to the Kreuzboden lift stop brings you to the starting point of many walks, with superb views across the Saas valley. (See Walk #5.)

6. Zermatt - Zermatt is a tourist and hiking mecca in the valley next to Saas-Fee. Its surrounding mountains and glaciers encompass superb scenery, including the mighty Matterhorn. The abundance of railroads and cable cars reaching the tops of Zermatt's high, snow-capped mountains makes this a perfect place for a day-trip from Saas-Fee. You can spend the day in Zermatt, with its trendy mix of souvenir shops and cosmopolitan boutiques, "in" restaurants and small cafes, or choose any of the following sightseeing options.

A. Gornergrat Cog Railway - (entrance across the street from the Zermatt Railroad station)

Gornergrat - 10,272 feet - 1 1/2 hours round-trip travel time. The highest rack railway in Europe brings *Easy Walkers* to Gornergrat, with a fabulous view of the Matterhorn, and the spectacular sight of the Monte Rosa and its glaciers, at 15,203 ft., the highest mountain in Switzerland.

Stockhorn - 11,588 ft. - 45-minute round-trip from the top station of the Gornergrat Railway.

The railway takes you from Zermatt at 5,315 ft., to Gornergrat at 10,272 ft., and *Easy Walkers* may continue by cable car to the Stockhorn peak at 11,588 ft. The first railway stop is at Riffelalp, where you will hike on another day. (See Walk #2 in the Zermatt section.) The last stop is Gornergrat, with the Kulm Hotel, a restaurant, and a large, outdoor terrace filled with skiers, hikers, climbers and sun-worshippers. *Easy Walkers* can continue to the Stockhorn peak by cable car for an awe-inspiring panorama.

B. Klein Matterhorn Cable Car - A 20-minute walk through Zermatt to the departure station. Turn right on leaving the railroad station, walk up the tourist-filled main street through town to the church, turn left, past the famous Zermatt cemetery. This well-tended cemetery, sitting in central Zermatt, serves as a testimonial to those climbers who lost their lives trying to scale the heights of the region's mountain peaks. The tombstones spell out the history and courage of men of all ages and countries, who tried to conquer the Matterhorn and failed.

As you pass the cemetery, cross the river and turn right at the Hotel Bristol, where a short walk toward the Matterhorn brings you to the lift station on your left.

Klein Matterhorn - 12,684 ft. - 2 hours round trip travel time. *Easy Walkers* will take four different and connecting cable cars to reach the top of the Klein Matterhorn, the highest altitude cable car station in Europe. The summer skiing on the Klein Matterhorn attracts people from around the world, and the view from France to Austria is breathtaking. Walkers can take advantage of the facilities at this station, including a cafeteria.

Schwarzsee - 8,500 ft. - change at the Furgg station of the Klein Matterhorn cable car for the 3-minute trip. The foot of the famed Matterhorn is your destination—its peak reflected in the still waters of a tiny mountain lake.

Sunnegga Underground Railway - After arriving in Zermatt, walk straight ahead and follow the sign to the Sunnegga Express Station.

Sunnegga - 7,500 ft. - Sunnegga sits on a high, alpine plateau, with a southwest view of the Matterhorn and panoramic vistas of mountains, glaciers, valleys, and lakes. The underground railway takes 20 minutes to reach the Sunnegga station. A restaurant and facilities are available for *Easy Walkers*, as well as many hiking trails. (See Walk #4 in the Zermatt section.)

Blauherd and UnterRothorn - From Sunnegga, a cable car continues up to Blauherd at 8,620 ft. where a second cable car takes riders to the rocky summit of the 10,180 ft. Unter-Rothorn, with its exceptional views of the Findel Glacier, the Matterhorn and Zermatt.

Directions to Zermatt: Take the early PTT bus from the Saas-Fee terminal to Stalden, and change for the train to Zermatt. For example: the 8:35 am bus from Saas-Fee arrives in Stalden at 9:15 am, and the train leaves Stalden at 9:49 am and arrives in Zermatt at 10:47 am. A 4:10 pm train from the Zermatt station brings you back to Saas-Fee at 6:20 pm, after changing in Stalden for the bus.

7. Kandersteg - This tiny town is built on a plateau, surrounded by rugged mountains and magnificent scenery. *Easy Walkers* will enjoy exploring Kandersteg, and perhaps sampling one of its many walks. The most popular is the chairlift and trail to the Oeschinensee, a blue glacial lake ringed by cliffs and the snow-covered Blumlisalp peaks.

Directions to Kandersteg: Take an early PTT bus from Saas-Fee to Brig and change for the train to Kandersteg. To return, take the train from Kandersteg to Brig, and change for the Saas-Fee bus.

8. Sion - Two craggy hills that appear to be borrowed from Disneyland, are the crowning glory of Sion, the capital of the Valais region. A ruined castle dominates one hill (Tourbillon), and a church dating back to the 11th century commands your attention on the second hill (Valère). These are only two of the indications of historical wealth to be found in the ancient streets of Sion. With the advent of the 20th century, Sion evolved into a produce center, its colorful and bustling markets contrasting magnificently with streets filled with a remarkable picture of medieval history.

Directions to Sion: Take an early bus from the PTT station in Saas-Fee to Brig. Change in Brig for the train heading west to Sion. To return, take the train from Sion to Brig, and change for the PTT bus to Saas-Fee.

9. Crans-Montana - The towns of Crans and Montana combined to fashion a resort complex on a sunny plateau at 5,000 ft. These side-by-side mountain villages offer visitors modern hotels and apartments, fashionable boutiques, swimming pools, tennis courts, golf courses, a casino and miles of scenic trails with several cable cars lifting *Easy Walkers* to the surrounding mountain peaks.

Directions to Crans-Montana: Take an early PTT bus from Saas-Fee to Brig, and change in Brig for a westbound train to Sierre. At the Sierre station, board a train or PTT bus to Crans/Montana. Check local timetables to see which is more convenient. To return to Saas-Fee, take the train or bus to Sierre, the train to Brig, and change for the Saas-Fee bus.

10. Leukerbad - Leukerbad is a well known name among spa aficionados in Europe. The town is set on a plateau at 4,600 ft., and is surrounded by mountains. Leukerbad's warm water springs are reputed to be the hottest in Switzerland, and many therapeutic properties are attributed to them. A variety of disorders are treated at the spas—gout, arthritis, muscle pulls and spinal injuries. A visit to Leukerbad was considered a must in the 1800s, and in Mark Twain's book, *Tramp Abroad,* he depicted various travelers and their ailments "taking the waters." *Easy Walkers* can take cable cars to Gemmi from Leukerbad.

Directions to Leukerbad: Take an early PTT bus from Saas-Fee to Brig, and change for the westbound train to Sierre. Change in Sierre for the PTT bus to Leukerbad. To return, take the PTT bus in Leukerbad to Sierre. In Sierre, take the train east to Brig, where you change for the PTT bus to Saas-Fee.

11. Sierre - Sierre boasts of being the driest and sunniest town in Switzerland—more than 200 days of sunshine and only 24 inches of rain a year. It has an old quarter with a 15th-century tower castle, a 13th-century tower house, and Chateau Bellevue, built in the 1600s as a miniature replica of Versailles. This charming town is in the heart of the Valais wine region, and the local tourist office can supply maps for walks through the vineyards.

Directions to Sierre: Take an early PTT bus from Saas-Fee to Brig, and change for the westbound train to Sierre. To return to Saas-Fee, take the eastbound train to Brig and change for the PTT bus.

12. Val D'Hérens Region - The city of Sion (see Excursion #8.) is the gateway to Val d'Hérens, one of the loveliest valleys leading off the Rhône River area. It is a 25-mile bus ride south to Arolla, with the road rising almost 5,000 ft. to the base of the 12,000 ft. Aguille de la Tsa. Ask the bus driver to let you off at Evolene, one mile above sea level, whose quaint main street is lined with 400 year-old wooden houses. Every location in Evolene offers magnificent views of the 14,304 ft. Dent Blanche, spectacular in its craggy appearance. Euseigne is another stop on the PTT bus, and its pyramids are each capped by a swaying boulder.

Directions to Val d'Hérens: Take an early PTT bus from Saas-Fee to Brig, and change for a westbound train to Sion. In Sion, catch the PTT bus heading south down the Val d'Hérens, with stops in Euseigne, Evolene, Les Haudères and Arolla. To return to Saas-Fee, take the PTT bus from any of the above villages to Sion, where you change for the train to Brig. In Brig, change for the PTT bus to Saas-Fee.

Saas-Fee Walks

Walk #1: Hannig to Hohnegg to Saas-Fee

Walking Time - 2 hours

Today's walk serves as a fine introduction to Saas-Fee and its surroundings—acquainting *Easy Walkers* with the flora and fauna at the Hannig lift station. This hike brings you back to your hotel early in the afternoon, leaving a few hours for sightseeing, shopping or other activities in Saas-Fee.

Directions: Buy your picnic lunch from any of the bakeries, cheese shops and meat markets along the way to the Hannig cable car—easily found and well-signed above the center of town. Purchase your one-way ticket, Saas-Fee to Hannig. The four-passenger cable cars run continuously and silently on this 2,500 ft. ascent, bringing hikers to a large sun-terrace with

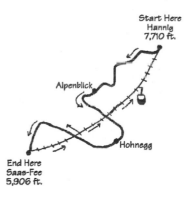

Start Here
Hannig
7,710 ft.

Alpenblick

Hohnegg

End Here
Saas-Fee
5,906 ft.

spectacular views. To your right is the famous Fee glacier, dominating the panorama around Saas-Fee. Other cable lifts are visible—Plattjen directly across the valley; another to Spielboden and Längfluh, going directly up the center of the Fee glacier. (See Walks #2 and #7.) A third lift rises to Felskinn, where visitors change for the famous Metro-

Alpin Subway, whisking *Easy Walkers* and summer skiers to Mittelallalin. (See Walk #3.) Saas-Fee, of course, is directly below you. The panorama from this viewpoint is breathtaking, making it easy to see that Saas-Fee is sitting on the stage of an amphitheater, with mountains and glaciers surrounding it on three sides.

Start: The familiar directional signs outside the lift station will highlight the myriad of walks from this location. Follow the path to "Saas-Fee" and "Hohnegg," walking left, facing the signs. The Fee glacier is directly ahead in all its frozen majesty as you begin to descend. In a few hundred yards the trail splits. Take the left path marked, "Saas-Fee," "Alpenblick," "Hohnegg." This is a comfortable, yellow-blazed trail, zigzagging to ease the level of descent. It is one of the most scenic paths in the area—giving *Easy Walkers* an understanding of why Saas-Fee is called "The Pearl of the Alps."

Within 30 minutes, a well-signed fork in the trail directs you to the right to Saas-Fee by way of "Hohnegg." Close any gates behind you—to keep the cows in the pasture—passing under a small ski lift, and continuing to follow the yellow blazes. In less than an hour you'll reach the Alpenblick Restaurant. Benches in this area afford magnificent views and are perfect picnic spots.

Continuing, use the left path to Hohnegg. You'll come to a four-way, unsigned trail junction—walk straight ahead to a sign reading, "Saas-Fee, Hohnegg." This trail is now a pleasant forest path—the earlier part of the walk was above the tree line. Pass a children's playground and picnic area on the left, and at another junction, turn right to "Saas-Fee." Almost immediately, another group of yellow signs directs you to the right to "Hohnegg, Saas-Fee." Tiny Hohnegg consists of a few restaurants and chalets, in a picturesque, alpine setting. The path continues down, parallel to Saas-Fee, toward the Felskinn cable car, bringing you into the outskirts of town. The afternoon is free to explore the side streets, the Sports Center with its indoor and outdoor activities, or visit the tiny Saaser Museum, just up from the church, with an entry fee of 3 SF. This museum will help *Easy Walkers* understand the development of this beautiful village and the surrounding Saas areas. One of the many tea rooms and patisseries can help ease any hunger pangs left from this exhilarating 1,700 ft. descent.

Walk #2: Spielboden to Saas-Fee

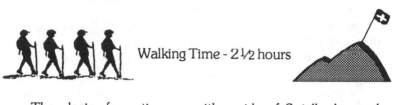

Walking Time - 2½ hours

The glacier formations on either side of Spielboden and Längfluh look like giant, frozen ice waves. A narrow finger of land juts up to form these two lift stations, and on this small area, surrounded on three sides by glaciers, are much-traveled hiking trails.

Directions: Buy the components for your picnic lunch. Walk down the main street, past the church, toward the Fee glacier, and look for the signs pointing to the "Längfluh-Spielboden Luftseilbahnen." These cable cars run continuously and

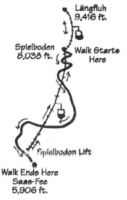

Längfluh
9,416 ft.

Spielboden
8,038 ft.

Walk Starts
Here

Spielboden Lift

Walk Ends Here
Saas-Fee
5,906 ft.

automatically. Purchase a one-way Saas-Fee to Spielboden ticket at the "Spielboden" window, step into the four-person car, and begin your ascent, looking down at the little town of Saas-Fee, growing smaller as the car rises. You'll spot many walking paths, with hikers feeding the ever-present colonies of tame marmots Spielboden is noted for. They are gentle animals and beg for food in a most beguiling manner.

Your walk begins at the Spielboden stop. It is above the tree line and on a tongue of land surrounded by two sides of the Fee glacier. Another cable car or a well-signed trail marked 1 hr. (plan on 1 1/2 hours), takes *Easy Walkers* up to Längfluh at 8,600 ft., and this is an option to exercise if the day is clear. Otherwise, meet the marmots at Spielboden, waiting patiently for your arrival. A walk to either side of this lift station brings you into view of the powerful Fee glacier, dominating the panorama around tiny Saas-Fee.

Start: The trail down from Spielboden begins with a sign directing hikers to Saas-Fee. It's a gradual descent, and even though there are little spin-offs on the path, we urge you to stay on the main, well-trodden trail. This route, marked with red and white blazes, is easy to travel—it zigzags often to ease the level of descent. As you continue towards Saas-Fee, marmot families may come out to greet you, their little burrows visible everywhere. Again, you'll find more hikers going up the mountain instead of down—Europeans prefer to walk up—and we can tell you that it's much easier on knees and toes!

Winding down the trail, you'll reach a fork next to a small stone house. Take the path to the left for a close-up view of the glacier—a fascinating scene worth this detour. After glacier gazing, return to the main path next to the stone house and continue down to Saas-Fee. Another sign directs walkers to "Saas-Fee" to the right, or "Saas-Fee" and "Cafe Gletschergarten" to the left. We recommend taking the left fork to the restaurant, where the many nice rock formations can be used for picnicking. At the restaurant, buttonhook to the right, following the trail to Saas-Fee. From this point, yellow blazes take you to "The Pearl of the Alps." Pass under the cable cars and cross over a stream on a small wooden bridge. Follow a wide road, and the Felskinn cable station comes into view. At the cable station there are a variety of paths to choose—all leading into Saas-Fee.

WALK #3: Felskinn to Britanniahütte to Felskinn (including excursion to Mittelallalin)

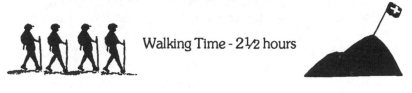

Walking Time - 2½ hours

This glacier walk at almost 10,000 ft. will emphasize the grandeur and scope of the walking trails surrounding Saas-Fee. You will travel by cable car to Felskinn, walk across the Chessjen glacier to the Britanniahütte, and walk back to Felskinn. The Britanniahütte flies the British flag as well as the Swiss, and was built in the early 1900s by British members of the Swiss Alpine Club. Local authorities continuously check the safety of the glacier path to the hut. This hike is particularly rewarding, and gives *Easy Walkers* a very different and exciting type of Swiss walking experience. Remember that sunscreen and sunglasses should be used at all times.

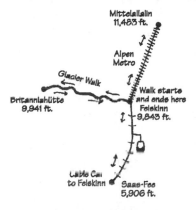

The excursion part of today's walk, the ride on the Metro Alpin, the world's highest subway, will allow *Easy Walkers* to emerge into the center of a glacial wilderness. Ride up for the view—it's unforgettable. (See Excursion #3B.)

Directions: Buy provisions for a picnic lunch and walk past the church on the main street of Saas-Fee, heading south, towards the imposing Fee glacier. The Felskinn cable car is on the other side of the tennis courts, about a 20-minute walk from the church. Follow the signs past the edge of town to the lift station marked "Felskinn" and buy a round-trip ticket to Mittelallalin. The smooth, fast ride up to Felskinn is in a large gondola that can hold up to 90 people, and deposits *Easy Walkers* at 9,800 ft., ready to begin their exciting glacier adventure.

Start: At Felskinn you have the option of continuing up to Mittelallalin, but we suggest you save this experience for after your walk and lunch. Leaving the lift station, follow the signs to the hut—over a snowfield and on to the glacier. This is not an easy hike, but the rewards are great. Use caution and be deliberate—at any given time (depending on temperature) the path can be slippery, slushy, rocky or muddy. Just remember to stay on the well-marked path, and use all ropes provided for walking help. As you proceed, you'll see deep, narrow glacial ravines—enjoy this incredible scenery and the fact that you're actually walking on a glacier at 10,000 ft.—quite an accomplishment! After about half an hour you'll come upon two small houses at a tiny ski lift at the Egginerjoch. The walk becomes more difficult after this point, so use your discretion to continue or to turn back. If you proceed to the hut, you'll be greeted with a warm welcome, a hot drink and bathroom facilities. To return to Felskinn, retrace your steps back across the glacier.

Many *Easy Walkers* decide to "glacier walk" as far as the ski lift, and enjoy their picnic lunch on this rocky outpost. Black alpine birds called *choughs* hover nearby, and enjoy the bread thrown to them—swooping down into this glacial wilderness to savor a delicious bit of civilization.

When you return to the Felskinn lift station, take the Metro-Alpin, the highest subway in the world, to Mittelallalin. The train cuts through the mountain, covering a distance of 1,300 ft. in only 3.2 minutes, disembarking passengers at a height of 11,342 ft. at the top station. This subway has made a new area of summer skiing available in the midst of a majestic mountain chain. The revolving restaurant is the highest in the world, rotating once an hour on its axis. A cafeteria is also on the site, with an exceptionally large sun-terrace—perfect for gazing at 6 impressive mountain peaks of over 12,000 ft.—and their majestic, snow-covered neighbors.

Return to Saas-Fee via the Metro-Alpin to Felskinn, taking the gondola from Felskinn back to the Saas-Fee station, where there are many paths leading into town.

Walk #4: Saas-Fee to Saas-Grund to Saas-Almagell (including excursion to Kreuzboden)

Walking Time - 4 hours

This walk includes the "Kappellenweg" (chapel path) to Saas-Grund. 15 tiny chapels—1687 to 1709—were built as a pilgrimage route from Saas-Fee, through the rocks, along the Feevispa River, and down into the valley between Saas-Grund and Saas-Almagell. This is a wonderful way for *Easy Walkers* to familiarize themselves with these little villages, and absorb the mountain and glacier scenery of the area.

Start: In Saas-Fee, pick up your picnic lunch and walk to the Postbus station. The path to Saas-Grund in back of the PTT

Start Here
Saas-Fee
5,906 ft.

Optional walk to Saas-Fee

End Here
Saas-Grund

Saas Almagell
5,059 ft.

Kreuzboden
7,865 ft.

station is marked "Kappellenweg." The 15 miniscule chapels along this route in the forest include one small church still holding services. Each chapel contains a group of carved and painted religious figures.

This path descends fairly steeply, but is well-trodden and easily followed. The valley, ravine and river are on the right and Saas-Fee is above on the left. About 10 minutes from the top, the church appears, and if you are fortunate enough to be walking on the Kappellenweg on Sunday morning, the choir is a harmonious addition to the birds singing in the forest. In some areas the path descends on stone steps. Walk carefully, making sure your hiking shoes are laced tightly. You'll probably find more people ascending than descending— most Europeans would rather walk up than down.

The descent is about 600 ft., but before the hour is over, the end of the trail appears. A sign points right to "Saas-Almagell," but turn left on the path and follow it along the river, past the campground on the left. Cross the bridge, turn left, and proceed toward Saas-Grund. Follow the signs, with a symbol of a chair lift, to the Kreuzboden cable car. (See Excursion #5.) Buy a round-trip lift ticket to Kreuzboden with its restaurant and sun-terrace, but if you've brought a picnic lunch, head for one of the most beautiful spots in the Swiss Alps. Walk around the restaurant to a miniature alpine lake with a tiny waterfall, breathtaking views of Saas-Fee and its surroundings and a rock-strewn pasture that can serve as your outdoor dining room.

A short, but interesting hike to the Hannig Panorama is marked for 20 minutes—it will probably take *Easy Walkers* 45 minutes, or 1 1/2 hours round-trip. The trail rises up and around the mountain, over a *very rocky path,* where deliberate caution should be exercised, ascending to a sightseeing point overlooking Hannig. This trail is demanding, and *Easy Walkers* should feel fit and rested before attempting it. Remember, if a trail begins to make you feel uncomfortable, return to the starting point.

When ready to leave Kreuzboden, take the cable car back down to Saas-Grund for the valley walk to Saas-Almagell. Retrace your steps to the end of the Kappellenweg path to the sign marked, "Saas-Almagell." This lovely path goes through the dozen houses of Unter den Bodmen, and wends its way along the river banks, going inland a few times to wind through meadow and forest to Saas-Almagell. The PTT stop is on the outskirts of town. Check the posted schedule before exploring the tiny town square or settling in for a delicious snack at the terrace restaurant conveniently situated by the bus stop. Take the PTT bus back to Saas-Grund, changing for the bus to Saas-Fee, although some buses do not require a change. Ask the bus driver.

Walk #5: Saas-Fee to Bideralp to Stafelalp to Saas-Fee

Walking Time - 5 hours

Today's walk is the most aggressive hike suggested, but it is a particularly beautiful excursion into the heights overlooking the Saas Valley. This walk offers many different kinds of alpine walking experiences—uphill, downhill and level; waterfall and stream crossings; rocky trails and pine needled paths—and an altitude change of over 1,000 ft.! The path is easy, wide, and carpeted with layers of pine needles for 1 hr., the ascent steepens and the trail becomes rocky. After the Biderbruche crossing, the trail rises again, ascending 1,000 ft., swings to the left and meets the high altitude trail from Grächen. It then descends by way of Bärenfalle, into the outskirts of Saas-Fee.

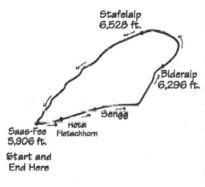

Stafelalp
6,528 ft.

Bideralp
6,296 ft.

Sengg

Saas-Fee   Hotel
5,906 ft.   Fletschhorn

Start and
End Here

Start: Remember to pack a picnic lunch—this is one of the few trail areas *without* a restaurant or facilities. Walk north on the main street, away from the Fee glacier, past the Hotels Allalin, Eden and Etoile. After passing the Alpen l litte restaurant, follow signs to the right directing walkers to the Fletschhorn Hotel and Restaurant. After about 10 minutes, pass through the charming Hotel Fletschhorn sunterrace, continuing on the other side. There will be signs marked "Stafelalp," "Bideralp" and "Sengg." Follow this path but ignore the fact that it's marked "Stafelalp - 1 hr., 15 minutes" It may take *Easy Walkers* 2 hours.

The road becomes a lovely, wide path, thickly carpeted with pine needles and very comfortable to walk on. It is also marked as a running path—part of the fitness course in the outskirts of Saas-Fee. As you proceed, the lift to Kreuzboden across the valley in Saas-Grund is in view. After half an hour, you'll pass through the tiny hamlet of Sengg. Enjoy the photographic possibilities in this area—it appears as though time and modern civilization have bypassed Sengg and its surrounding meadows. Walk through the village, following directions to "Stafelalp." The trail begins to climb in the direction of Bideralp and Stafelalp, as you cross swiftly-running streams. As you ascend, you'll come to a fork that is not signed, but on a large rock to the left, "Bideralp" is painted in large yellow letters, with an arrow pointing to the left fork. You've now walked about an hour and have come to a point where the trail becomes narrow and rocky, rising at a steeper rate. *Easy Walkers* have the option here of turning around and walking back to Saas-Fee on the same trail, leaving the afternoon free for other activities or excursions.

Continue, following this yellow painted sign to Bideralp, and in about 1 hour, you'll cross the fast-running Biderbruche on a small wooden bridge. You are now in Bideralp, with many scenic opportunities for a picnic. *Easy Walkers* should now be prepared to ascend almost 1,000 ft. on a well-traveled path. After passing some wooden cabins, the trail hairpins to the left around Stafelalp to meet the high altitude path coming down from Grachen. At the Grachen sign, you are at the highest point of this walk, and from then on it's downhill into Saas-Fee. *Easy Walkers*: you'll be fording streams and crossing waterfalls as you descend from a rocky mountain trail to a pine-needled forest path leading into Saas-Fee. The Swiss Alpine Club has placed guide ropes at some strategic spots on this descent. The return to Saas-Fee is on a different path than the morning trail—it's a higher level walk. Follow the signs to Saas-Fee, stay on the main path, rejecting all other options. After reaching Barenfalle, the outskirts of Saas-Fee soon appear.

If you leave your hotel by 10 am, you'll be back before 5 pm, after an exhilarating day of hiking.

Walk #6: Plattjen to Saas-Fee

Walking Time - 3 hours

The cable car to Plattjen offers another view of the mountains and glaciers encircling Saas-Fee. On the walk from Hannig to Saas-Fee, the Plattjen area was in full view across the valley. (See Walk #1.) Now, the Hannig/Mëllig area can be seen clearly, along with the Fee Glacier and the tall snow-covered peaks making up the Saas-Fee panorama. The impressive Mischabel mountain range is in full view from the top station, and the walk down from these heights is through pine and larch forests. Although the path can be steep—a total descent of over 2,000 ft.—*Easy Walkers* should experience no problems.

Directions: As you walk through town towards the Plattjen cable car, remember to pick up your picnic lunch. Head south, past the village church and toward the mountains, for about 20 minutes, to the Plattjen lift station. Buy your one-way ticket to Plattjen and take the gondola up to almost 8,000 ft. under the Mittaghorn, overlooking Saas-Fee. At the top, a restaurant and facilities are available.

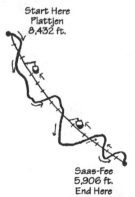

Start Here
Plattjen
8,432 ft.

Saas-Fee
5,906 ft.
End Here

Start: Follow the trail as it begins to descend beneath the cable cars. At the first fork, turn left and follow the path as it buttonhooks steeply. Stay on the main trail Saas-Fee, and don't be tempted by side paths as you through the forest, eventually coming to a wide wagon p Follow this road and then turn right, passing the lower car station, with signs directing you back to Saas-Fee.

ZERMATT

Zermatt, at 5,300 ft., is nestled among alpine meadows and pine forests, and is encircled by many of Switzerland's tallest and most famous mountains. Not much in this car-free, cosmopolitan city can be considered removed from the tourist scene, however the Zermatt area continues to be a hiker's paradise, encompassing some of the most superb scenery and appealing walking trails in the world. With a year-round population of about 4,000 residents that burgeons into tens of thousands in season, this sophisticated village in the Valais region of Switzerland, has two contrasting areas. One section includes the main street from the railroad station to the church—filled with day-trippers, skiers and hikers from all over the world—enjoying the chic boutiques, bustling restaurants and old-world hotels. The second area begins beyond the church and reaches into the countryside in the shadow of the high mountains, with typical Valasian chalets, and a network of trails to suit the needs of occasional ramblers and experienced mountain climbers.

French is the language spoken in the western Valais region of Switzerland, but nearing Brig, the sounds of a Germanic dialect begin, and the word "Valais" becomes "Wallis." The upper Valais was invaded after the 6th century by a Germanic people who pushed southward as far as Sion and Sierre. French is the language of choice in Champex, a lake village near the French border, while in Zermatt, also in the Valais or Wallis region, Swiss German (Schwyzer Deutsch) is spoken.

Zermatt is traffic-free, tourists dominating the streets—except early in the morning when a large herd of bearded goats takes over and trots through the main street, neck bells ringing noisily in the clear, mountain air. A giant car-park was built at the Täsch railroad station in the valley, to garage the cars of the thousands who visit Zermatt. This ban on cars is ecologically sound and allows visitors to wander through Zermatt's quaint streets with only darting, electric mini-taxis and flower-bedecked horse-drawn carriages for transportation.

Zermatt has become synonymous with the majestic Matterhorn, and while it is not the highest mountain in the Zermatt area, its silhouette and history are unique, and instantly recognizable to millions. The Matterhorn holds a hypnotic fascination for all who see it. In the 1860s, Edward Whymper, a young British illustrator, wandered through the Alps to conquer the high mountain peaks. He was fascinated by the Matterhorn and kept returning to Zermatt where he unsuccessfully attempted to climb this formidable peak eight times. On July 14, 1865, Whymper, three other British climbers and three guides, finally mastered the Matterhorn, but on their descent, a line snapped, and four of the men fell 4,000 ft. to their death. All are buried in the town cemetery, as are climbers of many nations, a testament to those who lost their lives climbing the Matterhorn and its surrounding peaks and ridges.

The Zermatt area has one of the finest networks of alpine walks in the Swiss Alps, and *Easy Walkers* should plan to spend at least a week exploring the trails, activities and excursions. This location also brings a marvelous bonus to photographers longing to catch the Matterhorn at sunrise, or to film pristine mountain lakes with high peaks reflected in still, blue waters.

Transportation

Geneva Airport to Zermatt - While waiting for your luggage to arrive, use the money exchange office conveniently located adjacent to the baggage carousels. After clearing Swiss customs, look for large signs marked "Gare," with a symbol of a train, and proceed to the railroad station within the Geneva airline terminal. Any ticket agent will validate your Swiss Card or Swiss Pass.

Trains run frequently for the short ride from Geneva airport to "Geneva Central," where you change for the train to Visp. *Easy Walkers* are reminded to look for railway cars clearly marked with a non-smoking symbol and a "2" for second class, if that is your preference. As you board the train, a seat on the right side, facing front, will bring good views of Lake Geneva and its charming old towns, while the left side offers vistas of the rolling hills covered with vineyards. After stops in Lausanne, Montreux and Martigny, the train heads east towards Visp, with snow-covered peaks gradually appearing closer on the horizon. At the Visp station, change for the train to Zermatt on the Brig-Visp-Zermatt Railway (BVZ), leaving 36 minutes past every hour. This is a rack, or cog railway, enabling the train to cope with steep grades.

The train begins its ascent from 2,165 ft., at the ancient village of Visp, to your Zermatt destination at 5,300 ft. The train ride from Visp to Zermatt is 1 hour and 10 minutes of incredible visual joy, as the tall peaks of the region come into view one by one. The little hamlet of St. Niklaus, with its onion-dome church topped by a near-east minaret-style clock tower, is the first stop, and soon you'll be passing through Randa, destroyed by glacier slides four times in the last 200 years. The countryside is terraced, with grapevines and orchards planted on every available piece of land without forests, but the lumber business earns money for many tiny villages in this area. The train winds its way into the small mountain village of Täsch with its enormous parking lot—the last place a driver can leave a car before arriving in Zermatt. If your hotel's electric cart is not waiting outside the large Zermatt railroad station, use the bank of telephones inside the station, directly connected to all hotels, and inform the hotel operator you are at the station and wish to be picked up. Small electric taxis are also available outside the station for the short ride to the many hotels and apartments in Zermatt.

If you are traveling to Zermatt from a place other than Geneva, remember that there is always a change of train in Brig or Visp. Check local timetables for best connections.

Sample Timetable:

Geneva Airport to Geneva Central	Take any train
Geneva	10:49 am dep.
Visp	12:12 pm arr.
Visp	12:36 pm dep.
Zermatt	13:47 pm arr. (1:47 pm)

Activities in Zermatt

This section lists activities available in Zermatt on days when additions or alternatives to walking are desired. The Zermatt Tourist Office is located diagonally across the street from the railroad station. Telephone number - 026 66 11 81.

- Tennis - 17 courts, 2 indoors
- Vita Parcours - keep fit course
- Mini-golf
- Horseback Riding
- Swimming - indoor, salt water pools and saunas
- Billiards
- Bowling
- Horse drawn carriage rides
- Ice skating - natural ice rink open 10 am to 6 pm daily
- Helicopter rides - call Air Zermatt at 028 67 34 87 for further information.
- Bird and animal watching - the Zermatt tourist bureau will supply maps showing the most likely places to see eagles, ibex, marmot, chamois and other rare alpine birds and animals.
- Alpine Museum - has a collection of documents verifying the first ascents of the mountains around Zermatt, including the most famous—the Matterhorn on July 14, 1865. This exhibit will enchant *Easy Walkers* interested in the history of mountaineering in Zermatt. Other exhibits include a variety of different rock types, an interesting collection of local butterflies and examples of local flora and fauna. Be sure to examine the two scale relief models. One is of the Matterhorn, the other is of the entire mountain system surrounding Zermatt.
- Alpine Cemetery - this well-tended, beautiful cemetery is across from the church and the river, and contains the graves of those hardy souls "killed while attempting to climb the Matterhorn" and other surrounding peaks.
- The Marmots' Fountain - In the center of Zermatt stands a sculpture by Swiss artist Edouard Marcel Sandoz. He felt that art should reflect love of nature, and after a long stay in Zermatt, he donated the fountain to local residents in 1946.

Excursions in and Around Zermatt

This section introduces day excursions for *Easy Walkers* to enjoy when the weather is not suitable for high-altitude walking, or an alternative to walking is desired. Be sure to check local timetables for best connections if using public transportation.

1. Gornergrat-Stockhorn (Zermatt) - The Gornergrat Railway, directly across from the Zermatt railroad station, brings *Easy Walkers* to one of the most popular observation points in the Swiss Alps. After stops at Riffelalp, Riffelberg and Rotenboden, the Gornergrat sun-terrace, at 10,170 ft., lives up to its reputation for a magnificent view—almost daring a writer to do it justice! Look east to the massive spectacle of the Monte Rosa, west to the familiar peak of the Matterhorn, and between them—half dozen glaciers sweeping past a dozen mountains over 12,000 ft. The cable car from Gornergat to the Stockhorn at 11,240 ft., is a continuation into the world of ice and snow, and should not be missed.

In the summer the Gornergrat Railway operates between 4:30 and 5:30 am. for a spectacular sunrise viewing. Check with the Zermatt Tourist Office for specific details.

Directions to Gornergrat/Stockhorn: Walk down the main street of Zermatt, towards the railroad station. The Gornergrat railway is directly across the street from the Zermatt Railway station.

2. Klein Matterhorn-Schwarzsee (Zermatt) - The cable car to the Klein Matterhorn is a 33-minute, four-stage system to the highest station in Europe. This top station is the starting point for Zermatt's summer skiing, but it is the incredible view that *Easy Walkers* will appreciate—from Mont Blanc in France to high peaks in Austria!

A change of cable car in Furi brings *Easy Walkers* to Schwarzsee in a few minutes. Schwarzsee is at the foot of the Matterhorn, whose peak is reflected in a small, crystal-clear, mountain lake. (See Walk #3.)

Directions to Klein Matterhorn/Schwarzsee: These lifts begin outside of Zermatt at the south side of town, and on the east side of the river. Follow the signs, turning left at the church, passing the cemetery, crossing the river and making an immediate right at the Hotel Bristol. The lift station is about a 10-minute walk along the river bank.

3. Sunnegga-Blauherd-Unterrothorn (Zermatt) - The silent, powerful, underground funicular "Alpen Metro" rises to the sunny Sunnegga plateau at 7,459 ft. From there, a gondola ascends to Blauherd at 8,530 ft., and a cable car continues to the Unterrothorn at 10,170 ft.

Directions to Sunnegga/Blauherd/Unterrothorn: The Sunnegga Express Station is on the east side of the river, close to the Zermatt railroad station. Follow the signs in Zermatt.

4. Glacier Express - The Glacier Express, called "the slowest express train in the world," rides the 167 miles between Zermatt and St. Moritz in grand style. The electrically powered train rolls over 291 bridges and viaducts and through 91 tunnels in 7 hours and 42 minutes. The Glacier Express departs daily from Zermatt at 10:10 am. Be sure to make reservations for assigned seats and lunch in the dining car. This can be done through a travel agent in Zermatt or the Swiss National Tourist Office in New York (212-757-5944) before you leave the United States.

5. Saas-Fee - Saas-Fee is a small, charming, car-free resort in the valley next to Zermatt, separated only by the Mischabel range of mountains. Directly outside of town are three chairlifts and the world's highest underground railway—Metro Alpin—transporting visitors to a wonderland of ice and snow.

A. Längfluh-Spielboden - The first stop on this cable car at Spielboden, brings *Easy Walkers* to a famous colony of tame marmots, begging to be fed. Both cable car stations are situated on a peninsula of land, splitting the Fee glacier, and are the beginning of many area walks. (See Walks and Excursions in Saas-Fee section.)

B. Felskinn-Mittelallalin - The station at Felskinn offers a fascinating view of the massive circle of peaks and glaciers surrounding Saas-Fee, and is the beginning of an exciting glacier walk to the Brittaniahutte. (See Walk #3 in Saas-Fee section.)

C. Hannig - The top station of this four-person cable car offers another panorama of the town of Saas-Fee and its encompassing glaciers and high peaks. (See Walk #1 and Excursion #3 in Saas-Fee section.)

D. Plattjen - This gondola lifts *Easy Walkers* to the heights of Plattjen, directly across from Hannig, with a splendid panorama of the Mischabel mountain range. (See Walk #7 and Excursion #4 in Saas-Fee section.)

Directions to Saas-Fee: Take the early train from the Zermatt railroad station to Stalden. Board the PTT bus to Saas-Fee outside the Stalden station. Check at the ticket window to see if bus reservations are needed. If necessary, make your return reservations at the bus station in Saas-Fee when you arrive in town.

6. Kandersteg - Situated at 3,860 ft., this all-season resort is built on a plateau and surrounded by rugged mountains and magnificent scenery. *Easy Walkers* will enjoy exploring Kandersteg and sampling its walks—one of the most famous is the chairlift and trail to Lake Oeschinen—a glacial lake surrounded by jagged cliffs and the snow-capped Blümlisalp peaks. (See Excursion #1 in Kandersteg section.)

Directions to Kandersteg: Take the early train from Zermatt to Brig and change for the train to Kandersteg. To return, take the train from Kandersteg to Brig and change for the train to Zermatt.

7. Sion - Sion, the 2,000 year old capital of the Valais region, is dominated by two steep hills that appear to be apparitions from Disneyland. A ruined castle is on one hill (Tourbillon), and a Gothic church is on the second hill (Valère), both dating back to the 12th and 13th centuries, and are an indication of the historical wealth to be found in Sion's ancient streets. Today the town is an agricultural center, its colorful and bustling markets contrasting magnificently with its sense of medieval history.

Directions to Sion: Take an early train from Zermatt to Visp, and change for the train heading west to Sion. To return, take the train from Sion to Visp and catch any train to Zermatt, leaving at 36 minutes past each hour.

8. Lugano - Lugano has been called, "the Rio de Janeiro of the old world," flowers, palm trees and tropical plants blooming around its lake shores. The large, clear lake, half in Switzerland and half in Italy, is a natural setting for the snow-capped mountains in the background. Explore Lugano's old arcades, narrow streets, fashionable boutiques and gourmet restaurants. Take a lake steamer for a short trip to picturesque towns like Gandria or Morcote. A small city near the Italian border, Lugano provides an interesting contrast to the icy glaciers and high mountains surrounding Zermatt.

Directions to Lugano: From June through September there is usually a once-a-week direct round-trip excursion from Zermatt to Lugano. Check with the Zermatt Tourist Office for details. If this train is not running, the ticket agents at the railroad station will help you with the most direct routing. *Easy Walkers* should remember however, that this is a full day's outing—leaving about 7 am and returning about 7 pm.

9. Crans-Montana - Crans-Montana is reached from Sierre, 9 miles to the south. A resort complex on a sunny plateau at 5,000 ft., Crans and Montana are side-by-side towns with modern hotels, apartments and fashionable stores, catering to a very celebrity-conscious clientele. They come to use the scenic trails, to swim, ride, play tennis or attend the Swiss Open Golf Championship. This vacation area boasts a 9 and 18-hole golf course, a casino and several cable car lifts.

Directions to Crans-Montana: Take the train from Zermatt to Visp, and change for the train to Sierre. At the Sierre station, take the PTT bus or funicular to Crans/Montana. To return to Zermatt, take the bus or funicular to Sierre, the train to Visp and then change for the Zermatt train. You might want to take the bus one way and the funicular back. Check schedules.

10. Sierre - Sierre claims the title of sunniest and driest town in Switzerland, with more than 200 days of sunshine and only 24 inches of rain a year. Its "old quarter" boasts a 15th-century tower castle, a 13th-century tower house and a miniature replica of Versailles, built in the 1600s. This charming town is in the heart of the Valais winemaking region, and the local tourist office will supply maps to visitors for hikes through the vineyards.

Directions to Sierre: Take an early train from Zermatt to Visp, and change for the westbound train to Sierre. To return to Zermatt, take the eastbound train to Visp and change for the Zermatt train.

11. Val d'Hérens Region (Hérens Valley) - One of the loveliest valleys leading from the Rhône River, Val d'Hérens is reached from the city of Sion. (See Excursion #7.) Twenty five miles south of Sion by PTT bus is the hamlet of Arolla, at the base of Mont Collon, and the last stop on this bus. Before reaching Arolla, *Easy Walkers* can get off at Evolène, a small town a mile above sea level, whose quaint main street is lined with 400 year-old brown, wooden houses. Every location in tiny Evolène offers magnificent views of the craggy and spectacular 14,304 ft. Dent Blanche. Euseigne, with its mushroom-shaped pyramids, is another interesting stop on the bus.

Directions to Val d'Hérens: Take an early train from Zermatt to Visp, and change for a westbound train stopping in Sion. Change in Sion for the PTT bus traveling into the Val d'Hérens region and making stops in Vex, Euseigne, Evolène, Les Haudères and Arolla. To return to Zermatt, take the PTT bus to Sion and change for the eastbound train to Visp. In Visp, change for the train to Zermatt.

12. Leukerbad - This spa, or "bad," is set at 4,600 ft. in a huge punchbowl with surrounding mountains. Leukerbad's warm water springs are reputed to be the hottest in Switzerland, and many therapeutic properties are attributed to them. Arthritis, disc injuries, muscle disorders and gout are among the ailments treated at this resort. In the 19th century, a visit to this spa was considered a must for travelers, and Mark Twain depicted these people in his book, *Tramp Abroad*. There are a variety of pools, each one having different healing qualities, and you can swim indoors or outdoors while "taking the waters." From Leukerbad, *Easy Walkers* can take a cable car to Gemmi, high above the spa, with great views of the region.

Directions to Leukerbad: Take an early train from Zermatt to Visp and change for the train to Sierre. Change in Sierre for the PTT bus to Leukerbad. To return to Zermatt, take the bus from Leukerbad to Sierre, and change for the train to Visp. In Visp, catch the Zermatt train leaving at 36 minutes past each hour.

13. Milan, Italy - Milan, with almost 1.75 million people, is first in Italian industry and business. However, *Easy Walkers* should not overlook its sightseeing pleasures. The Cathedral, begun in 1386 and finished in 1809, is a marvelous sight and is second only to St. Peters in Rome in size. Take an elevator to its roof for a spectacular view of Milan and the surrounding countryside. La Scala is the most famous opera house in the world, and has perfect acoustics. The Brera Palace and Picture Gallery is a 17th-century palace with works by Tintoretto, Veronese, Tiepolo, Raphael, El Greco, Rembrandt, Rubens and others. There are enough museums, churches and palaces to fill several days of Milanese sightseeing. We suggest a one-day trip to Milan to whet your appetite for a future walking trip in Italy and another visit to Milan.

Directions to Milan: Take the early train from Zermatt to Brig, and change for the train to Milan. The 7:10 am train from Zermatt arrives in Brig at 8:34 am, and the train departs Brig at 9:34 am, arriving in Milan at 11:45 am. The 4:10 pm train from Milan arrives in Brig at 6:28 pm, leaves Brig at 7:23 pm, and arrives in Zermatt at 8:47 pm. This is a full day's excursion, with only 4 hours to spend sightseeing, but the trip is through fascinating countryside in both Switzerland and Italy. **Remember to take your passport!**

14. Stresa, Italy - This beautiful Italian village is situated on the west bank of Lake Maggiore and faces the incredible Borromean Islands. Stresa has many 18th-century villas and gardens, and is pleasantly cool in summer because of its lakeside location. The Borromean Islands are world famous and should not be missed. The most famous is Isola Bella (Beautiful Island). There are guided tours through its extraordinary palace and gardens, and the view from the top terrace is breathtaking. Tiny Isola dei Pescatori (Fishermen's Island), preserves the original atmosphere of an old fishing village, with its narrow alleys and lake-front esplanade, and Isola Madre (Mother Island), contains an 18th-century palace and impressive gardens.

Directions to Stresa: In summer, a tour leaves every Wednesday from Zermatt to Stresa, with lunch and admission to the Borromean Islands included in the price. Information and reservations can be made at the Zermatt Railroad station. **Remember to take your passport!**

Zermatt Walks

Walk #1: Zermatt to Zmutt to Furi

 Walking Time - 3 1/2 hours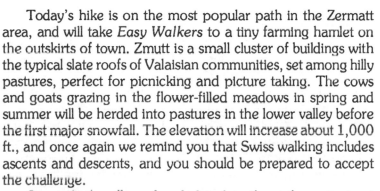

Today's hike is on the most popular path in the Zermatt area, and will take *Easy Walkers* to a tiny farming hamlet on the outskirts of town. Zmutt is a small cluster of buildings with the typical slate roofs of Valaisian communities, set among hilly pastures, perfect for picnicking and picture taking. The cows and goats grazing in the flower-filled meadows in spring and summer will be herded into pastures in the lower valley before the first major snowfall. The elevation will increase about 1,000 ft., and once again we remind you that Swiss walking includes ascents and descents, and you should be prepared to accept the challenge.

Start: At the village church, head south, up the main street toward the Matterhorn, past a bakery and butcher shop, where your picnic lunch can be purchased. As you pass a paper stand on your right, you'll see a sign indicating many different walk options. Continue straight ahead on the paved road that indicates "Zmutt - 1 hr." There are several ways to approach Zmutt—we prefer following the well-trodden path marked "1 hr.," although it may take *Easy Walkers* 1 1/2 hours. As you ascend, the river is on the left, the Matterhorn straight ahead.

Interestingly, you'll pass some barns from the early years of Zermatt—old wooden structures called *mazots*. These huts

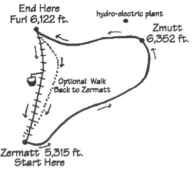

were used for storing feed for the livestock, and have round discs on the pedestals to keep rodents from getting inside. Fortunately, a few dozen of these wonderful antique barns have been preserved in the heart of Zermatt as well as its outlying areas, and help maintain the picturesque and historical beauty of this Valais region.

Proceed straight ahead on the main path to Zmutt. The path seems to head directly towards the Matterhorn, but the asphalt ends and you ascend gently on a mule path through woods and meadows. On the left is a steady flow of cable cars rising to Furi. This path continues to be well-signed, as you progress steadily up toward Zmutt. It's heartening to see mature citizens from all over the world—some with physical handicaps—walking with measured pace towards their objective for the day. Notice small pastures on your left where marmots have made homes, and watch these playful creatures frolicking outside their burrows. At a fork in the road, continue on the right hand path to Zmutt. Shortly, the Furi cable station will come into view across the ravine to your left. Stop for a moment, turn around and look to the north—see the railroad cars climbing up the mountain towards Gornergrat—looking like toy choochoos in a department store display!

The road buttonhooks sharply to the right. There is usually a little goat with an ever-clanging bell around his neck, waiting patiently at this curve for a sympathetic walker to provide lunch for him. You're very close to Zmutt now, and in a few minutes you'll walk right through the terrace of a restaurant sitting on the trail. Zmutt is only a 5-minute walk through the meadow, with its miniature whitewashed church, some old barns and houses and a few restaurants. The pasture is covered with wild flowers from June through August, and is an idyllic place to enjoy a picnic lunch. If you decided not to bring lunch, any one of the restaurants in Zmutt can provide a hearty, but more expensive alternative. From a picnic vantage point in a high meadow, gaze down on the old slate roofs of Zmutt, the valley and the peak of the Matterhorn. These Zmutt meadows gave their name to the Matterhorn, which means "meadow-horn" in the local dialect.

After lunch, take the path into the center of town and follow a sign down the hill toward "Furi" and "Stafelalp," walking through a pasture toward the huge hydroelectric plant, with the gorge on your left. Cross the wooden bridge, walk up the hill to the road, and turn left to Furi. Stay on this road and ignore the path cutting off to "Zum See," unless you wish to return to Zermatt this longer way. In 1/2 hr., on a gently descending paved road through the forest, you'll see the cable station at Furi.

At Furi, *Easy Walkers* have 2 options: continue the hike, following the signs to "Zermatt - 1 1/2 hours" or take the cable car from Furi down to Zermatt.

Walk #2: Riffelalp to Zermatt (includes excursion to Gornergrat and Stockhorn)

 Walking Time - 2 1/4 hours

Although today's walk is from Riffelalp to Zermatt, we first include an excursion to Gornergrat and the Stockhorn. (See Excursion #1.) To see the panorama unfold at Gornergrat is to experience a spectacular view of awesome mountains and ice-world glaciers that defies description. In fact, this view is so incredible that the excursion and walk should be taken on the first clear day. From the Gornergrat station, the train winds its way up steeply, passing the Riffelalp Station where we will begin our walk later in the day. Views of the Matterhorn and other area mountains are visible from both sides of the railroad cars.

There are other intermediate stops at Riffelberg and Roten-boden. The view from Gornergrat is a spectacular panorama of 27 peaks higher than 12,000 ft. Looming over this frozen sea of ice is the awesome Monte Rosa at 15,203 ft. From Gornergrat, a gondola brings you to the Stockhorn at 11,588 ft., and an even closer view of the Monte Rosa and the sur-rounding glacial wilderness. Eventually you'll return to the Gornergrat railway, taking it down to Riffelalp for the walk to Zermatt. *Easy Walkers* will probably consider today's excursion and hike one of the more memorable events in their trip.

Directions: Leave your hotel and walk down the main street of Zermatt towards the railroad station, picking up a pic-nic lunch and proceeding to the Gornergratbahn, located direct-ly across the street from the main railroad station. Buy a round-trip ticket, Zermatt to Stockhorn. This cog, or rack rail-way, leaves every 24 minutes for a 43-minute ride to the top.

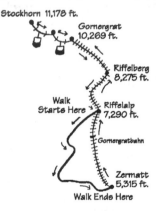

The scenery is spectacular from either side of the train, which makes three quick stops before arriving at Gornergrat. Board the wait-ing cable car immediately. If you feel a bit lightheaded at the Stockhorn station, move slowly and you'll soon adjust to the altitude. We know you remembered to stow a jacket in your backpack. There are no restaurants or facilities at the Stockhorn station.

Take the cable car—which runs every 24 minutes—back to Gornergrat and its famous Kulmhotel. Flat rocks outside the sun-terrace afford *Easy Walkers* a picnic with a view, and the black alpine choughs hover and swoop to catch bits of bread thrown for their lunch. You'll want to remember this array of glaciers and snow-capped mountains long after you return home. Just reading their names conjures fascinating images of the area's peaks: Monte Rosa, Liskamm, Castor, Pollux, Breithorn, Klein Matterhorn, Weisshorn, Matterhorn.

Reboard the train at Gornergrat and get off at the 6,600 ft. Riffelalp station, the stop after Riffelberg. Don't get them confused or your walk will be lengthened considerably.

Start: At the Riffelalp station, walk right, toward "Zermatt." Within a few minutes signs point to "Riffelalp" and "Zermatt." Do not take a path marked "Zermatt" to the right. Continue straight ahead on the main forest path, and within 10 minutes, the Hotel Riffelalp, with an unobstructed view of the Matterhorn comes into view. We suggest you stop for about an hour, ostensibly for a drink or dessert, but mainly to absorb the beauty of this incomparable view. Rooms with demi-pension at this hotel are about 200 SF per night for two—a perfect romantic hideaway for junior or senior walkers! After leaving the hotel, follow the path to "Zermatt" and "Winkelmatten." This trail descends at a steeper rate, so take it slowly and make sure your hiking boots are well-laced. The path divides at a restaurant—follow the right fork in back of the restaurant till you reach a paved mountain bike path. Turn right to Zermatt. This mountain bike path winds through the woods to the tiny hamlet of Winkelmatten, under the Sunnegga cable car, along the river and into Zermatt.

Walk #3:   Schwarzsee to Furi
(includes excursion to Klein Matterhorn)

 Walking Time - 2 hours

This trip takes *Easy Walkers* on an exciting excursion by a series of cable cars to the Klein Matterhorn at 12,533 ft., and a return to the Furi cable station for a short ride to Schwarzsee, where the walk begins. The cable car to Klein Matterhorn is a 33-minute, four-stage system: Zermatt to Furi; Furi to Furgg, riding above steep, rocky slopes and over alpine meadows;

Furgg to Trockener Steg, gliding over barren landscape till the glacier appears with its icy peaks; and Trockener Steg over the glacier to the Klein Matterhorn, the highest cable station in Europe. To reach Schwarzsee, return to Furgg and change for the Schwarzsee cable car. **Reminder to *Easy Walkers*:** Sunglasses and sunscreen are **essential** protection against the intense glare reflected from the glacier at Klein Matterhorn, and an insulated jacket can keep you warm at the peak. Enjoy the view from the top—this world of snow, ice and rock hasn't changed since the glaciers of the ice age destroyed everything in their paths.

Schwarzsee is at the foot of the Matterhorn, a tiny alpine lake below its northeast ridge. Mountain climbers trek from Schwarzsee to the Hornlihütte, now the base camp for mountaineers attempting to climb the Matterhorn. A miniature chapel with an interesting history was built at Schwarzsee to fulfill a vow made when a group of men became lost in a heavy snowstorm as they were crossing from Italy to Switzerland. They promised to dedicate a chapel to the Virgin Mary if they were saved, and at that moment the snow and clouds disappeared and the travelers were able to continue down to their destination in Zermatt. On a clear day the mountain lake mirrors the images of the nearby peaks and the chapel of St. Mary of the Snow. Photographers will be tempted to stay for hours! Be prepared to spend the bulk of the day on this trip, so pack a picnic lunch unless you wish to avail yourself of the restaurants at the Klein Matterhorn and along the trail.

Directions: The Klein Matterhorn cable car is about a 15-minute walk from the church. Follow the road between the church and the cemetery, cross the river, and make a right at the Hotel Bristol. Follow the signs to the lift station. Buy a lift ticket from Zermatt to Klein Matterhorn, with a return from Klein Matterhorn to Schwarzsee. Furi is the first stop—disembark and follow the signs to Klein Matterhorn. Keep your ticket handy and enter a larger cable lift to Furgg, and change again for Trockener Steg. Trockener Steg is the last change before your final stop at Klein Matterhorn. Summer skiing is a major sport in this area, and the lifts are filled with skiers from around the world. **Due to the altitude, move slowly, and use the jackets stowed in your backpack.** After disembarking at the Klein Matterhorn station, move ahead through a long tunnel. Half-way through this tunnel, on the left, is another small tunnel taking you up to the peak by elevator. A few steps further and you'll encounter a never-to-be-forgotten panorama. You'll be face-to-face with the Matterhorn, look across to the Stockhorn above Gornergrat, and see the Monte Rosa, Switzerland's tallest mountain. All around are the nearby glaciers, the far away peaks of the Bernese Oberland—the Eiger, the Mönch, the Jungfrau—and Mont Blanc in France.

When ready to leave, walk back through the tunnel and reverse the cable car procedure to "Schwarzsee."

Start: Pick up the descending trail to Furi down the front of the mountain, as indicated to "Hermettji" and "Zermatt - 2 1/2 hours" There are other ways to descend, but we recommend staying on this trail. It's clearly marked, wide, but rocky, and should present no problems to *Easy Walkers*. At the first fork, take a left into Hermettji. At Hermettji, take the first right, and then another right, following the signs to "Furi."

At the cable station in Furi, three options are available:

1. Take the cable car from Furi to Zermatt.

2. Continue the walk down to Zermatt by following the sign "Zermatt - 1 1/2 hours."

3. Walk to the Glacier Garden and back, then take the cable car from Furi to Zermatt.

Walk #4: Riffelalp to Grünsee to Findeln to Sunnegga

 Walking Time - 4 hours

Today's hike will take *Easy Walkers* on the Gornergrat Railway to Riffelalp for the start of the walk to Grünsee, a tiny glacial lake east of the Riffelalp stop. From Grünsee you'll walk down through the forest, and up to the tiny hamlet of Findeln, with its old wooden barns and houses. There are restaurants in Findeln, but a picnic lunch at the lake or in the meadows surrounding Findeln is a fine rest and relaxation stop. The walk will continue on an ascending path from Findeln to Lake Leisee, and eventually up to Sunnegga, with a return to Zermatt via the underground funicular. The last half of this walk is more aggressive, requiring some challenging, uphill walking.

Directions: After picking up picnic provisions, walk to the Gornergratbahn, across the street from the Zermatt station. Buy a one-way ticket, Zermatt to Riffelalp. Trains leave every 24 minutes for the 20-minute ride to Riffelalp. (See Excursion #1.) Detrain at the Riffelalp station.

Start: Walk across the railroad tracks at the pedestrian crossing—following the trail signed "Grünsee - 1 hr." This path is wide and well marked, winding around the mountain and offering superb views of the tiny towns in the valley below. You are at 6,500 ft. and slowly approaching the tree line. We took this walk in September when the colorful blooms of the wild flowers were replaced by the softer hues of dried pods. You'll soon see the great Findelgletscher to the east, and on the left, Sunnegga and the Blauherd-Unterrothorn lifts. (See Excursion #3.) Continuing on the path, take the right fork up the hill to Grünsee. The Findelgletscher and its surrounding peaks are now in front of you. Passing over a brook, a sign directs you to "Grünsee - 15 min." The "Barghus Findelgletscher" restaurant and facilities are on the left. Continue walking to "Grünsee - 3 min."

After enjoying the breathtaking panorama of lakes, mountains and glaciers from Grünsee, follow the same trail back, past the restaurant, and note the sign, "Findeln - 3/4 hr.," on a right fork in the path. You have the option of taking the left fork back to Riffelalp station—the same way you walked to Grünsee—and returning to Zermatt by train, or following the path to Findeln.

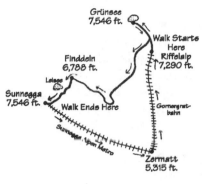

Grünsee
7,546 ft.

Walk Starts
Here
Riffelalp
7,290 ft.

Finddeln
6,788 ft.

Leisee

Sunnegga
7,546 ft.

Walk Ends Here

Gornergrat-
bahn

Sunnegga Alpen Metro

Zermatt
5,315 ft.

This trail winds through the forest and descends rapidly but comfortably to the Findelnbach (Findeln River). Look for herds of gentle, black-nosed sheep grazing lazily along the rocky path. Reaching the gorge and the Findelnbach, *Easy Walkers* again have an option. You can turn left (not crossing the bridge), following a narrow path slanting uphill through the pine forests, crossing a stream, descending steeply to the Gornergrat Findelnbach railroad station, and return to Zermatt via the Gornergrat railway.

Or, you continue by crossing the bridge and walking up the steepening path to Findeln. Climb slowly, shortly reaching the hillside hamlet of Findeln, perched on the side of the gorge. A restaurant, "Enzo's Hitte," is situated on the path. Turn right and continue up past the "Restaurant Alpenheim," with waitresses in traditional costumes. These restaurants serve lunch, but the outskirts of Findeln also has many nice picnic areas.

Continue on the steadily ascending path, walking on the well-signed trail above the town, till you come to a junction. Turn left for a short, aggressive, uphill walk to Lake Leisee, noticing the Sunnegga lift station above, on the hill. From the lake, take either of two paths leading to the top, and within a few minutes you'll be at the funicular subway which runs to Zermatt every 15 minutes. Buy a one-way Sunnegga-Zermatt ticket.

Walk #5: Sunnegga to Lake Leisee to Findeln to Findelnbach

Walking Time - 2 1/2 hours

The Matterhorn can be photographed from hundreds of hiking areas around Zermatt, but one of the best views is from the tiny hamlet of Findeln, where you'll walk today. This hamlet of old, slate-roofed farmhouses and wooden barns provides near-perfect images of the north and east faces of the Matterhorn. *Easy Walkers* will reach Findeln by way of the underground funicular to Sunnegga, continuing the walk via the Leisee.

Directions: After purchasing your picnic lunch, follow signs to Sunnegga, on the east side of the Visp River flowing through Zermatt. Buy a one-way Zermatt to Sunnegga ticket for the 7-minute ride. A restaurant and facilities are available at the top.

Start: Follow a path underneath Sunnegga and to the left, down to the Leisee. The path is above the tree line at this point, and cuts across the meadow surrounding the lake. At a trail junction, turn right and walk to Eggen, consisting of a few old wooden barns and houses. Walk downhill past old barns and through the pastures to Findeln.

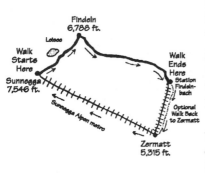

In the center of Findeln, turn left, descending downhill toward a wooden bridge. Cross the bridge and turn right on a narrow trail ascending through the dense forest. After crossing a stream, the trail descends rather steeply till you reach the Findelnbach station of the Gornergrat railway. The trains run every 24 minutes for the 7-minute ride to Zermatt. Buy a one-way ticket, Findelnbach to Zermatt. When you disembark, you'll be at the Gornergratbahn, across the street from the Zermatt train station.

Walk #6: Sunnegga to Tuftern to Reid to Zermatt

Walking Time - 3 hours

Today's walk is on another of the many trails leading from the Sunnegga plateau, primarily a forest path with an easy, 2,000 ft. descent with spectacular views of Zermatt and the Matterhorn. The underground Alpen-Metro funicular brings *Easy Walkers* to Sunnegga at 7,497 ft., and to the edge of a plateau with a magnificent panorama of the Matterhorn and other mountains and glaciers surrounding Zermatt. A cable car continues to Blauherd at 8,459 ft., and to the flat, rocky Unterrothern at 10,180 ft., where the view stretches southwest to the Matterhorn, south to the Findel Glacier, west to Zermatt, and north to the Nikolaital.

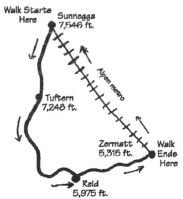

Directions: Pick up a picnic lunch, walking through Zermatt to the Sunnegga Alpen-Metro. Buy a one-way ticket, Zermatt to Sunnegga for the 7-minute ride on the underground funicular. At Sunnegga you emerge and go above ground to a lovely alpine plateau overlooking tiny Leisee, and the huge panorama of glaciers and mountains surrounding Zermatt. Take advantage of the restaurant and facilities at Sunnegga.

Start: Following the path to "Tuftern," head into the valley, away from the Sunnegga station. The hamlet of Tuftern consists of a small group of barns and houses, just above the tree line. Ignoring the right and left paths in Tuftern, continue on the well-marked trail to "Reid." This path descends gradually, buttonhooking back and forth through the forest and alpine meadows. In Reid, continue straight ahead, following the signs to "Haueten," to pick up the path into Zermatt, bringing walkers into the northeastern section of town.

CHAMPEX

The tranquil mountain resort of Champex is reached by a steep road, zigzagging up from the quaint market town of Orsières. The road climbs 1,877 ft. in 4 1/2 miles, hairpin turns snaking sharply back and forth, till it reaches this small, secluded village and lake, set in a mountain hollow, encircled by high, snow-covered peaks, and surrounded by flower-garlanded chalets and hotels. *Easy Walkers* will enjoy the clear mountain air in one of the prettiest and least-known resort areas in the Valaisian Alps. Champex, at 4,806 feet, is usually bypassed by tourists on their way to the nearby Hospice of Saint Bernard. In fact, many native Swiss are unaware of the unspoiled countryside and magnificent hiking areas around Champex.

Champex, situated in the canton of Valais, lies in the valley of the upper Rhone River. "Valais" is French, while "Wallis" is German, named for an area that was called "Vallis Poenina" by the Romans, meaning the upper Rhone valley. This region is Switzerland's third largest canton, but has a total population of less than 250,000 people. The western end closest to Lake Geneva is French-speaking, the eastern and upper end of the valley is German-speaking, with an interchange between the two languages occurring around Sion and Sierre, where some people speak in a dialect that is part French and part German, with a little Italian thrown in for flavor! This Valais region is composed of more than 50 formidable mountains, and is home to the largest glacier in Switzerland, but because the mountains act as a buffer, a combination of sun and even temperatures help make the Valais region a wine-producing area. The Valais vineyards produce Switzerland's red Dôle wine, white Fendant and the famous Williamine pear brandy.

Champex is located a short distance above the busy road to the Great Saint Bernard Pass, connecting the Drance and Dora Baltea valleys. This pass, linking Switzerland to Italy, is an ancient mountain crossing. However, in 1964 the Great Saint Bernard Tunnel was opened, and the need to use the pass diminished—except to visit the Saint Bernard Hospice, where monks have rescued stranded travelers for nine centuries. The famous Grand Saint Bernard dogs who accompanied the monks on their rescue missions may now be seen in the kennels behind the hotel. Modern-day helicopters, taking the place of these big, beautiful animals, now track down travelers in need of help.

The local Tourist Bureau reports that the sun shines on Champex all year long—a fact that walking enthusiasts will come to know and appreciate. Champex, on its miniature lake at the head of a deep wooded valley, is a gem. *Easy Walkers* can hire a paddle boat and leisurely explore the lake, fish for the famous trout, or just sit and absorb the peaceful serenity of water, woods and mountains. Walking on surrounding trails can be a stroll around the lake or a more strenuous hike into the mountains. Flower enthusiasts will be delighted with the nearby "l'Alpine Jardin Florealpe," an alpine garden with over 4,000 different plants growing in their native environment. Adventurous walkers can enjoy streams trickling down the sides of mountains, alpine pastures covered with flowers, and rural communities in the unspoiled countryside—all waiting to be discovered.

Transportation

Geneva Airport to Champex - After clearing Swiss customs, look for large signs marked "Gare" with a symbol of a train, and proceed to the railroad station within the Geneva airline terminal. As you walk into the station area, ticket windows are on the right and any agent will validate your Swiss Pass or Swiss Card. It is important to do this on your first and last days in Switzerland.

Trains run frequently between Geneva Airport and Geneva Central (the main city railroad station). Take the first train into Geneva Central and change for the train to Martigny—Brig is its final destination. As you board the train in Geneva Central, a seat on the right side, facing front, will bring good views of Lake Geneva (Lac Léman) and its charming, old towns. The left side offers vistas of rolling hills and vineyards, planted with grapes for local wines.

After stops in Lausanne, Vevey, Montreux and other beautiful lakeside towns, disembark in Martigny, descend the steps, cross under the train tracks, and walk up the steps to the Orsières train.

The train from Martigny to Orsières takes about half an hour. If you have to wait at the Orsières station for the bus to Champex, note an outdoor cafe at the hotel, left of the station. Or, walk straight ahead—to the left you'll find a small supermarket, a bakery filled with luscious pastries and a tiny outdoor cafe where it is *de rigeur* to buy pastry at the bakery and sit at a café table. Order a *café* or *thé* until the bus to Champex arrives. The 20-minute ride to Champex is steep and winding, leaving walkers exhilarated—anticipating their hiking adventures in Champex.

If you are traveling to Champex from a place other than Geneva, there is a change of train in Martigny going to Orsières, followed by a bus from Orsières to Champex. Check timetables.

Sample Timetable:

Geneva Airport to Geneva Central	Take any train
Geneva Central to Martigny	10:48 am dep.
Martigny	12:46 pm arr.
Martigny to Orsières	12:55 pm dep.
Orsières	13:25 pm arr. (1:25 pm)
Orsières to Champex (bus)	13:30 pm dep. (1:30 pm)
Champex	13:52 pm arr. (1:52 pm)

Activities in Champex

This section lists activities available in Champex on days when additions or alternatives to walking are desired. The Champex Tourist Office is on the main street near the small supermarket.

- Swimming - outdoor heated pool east of the village is open from June to September. Phone 83 26 52 for information.
- Tennis - two clay courts—one is next to the swimming pool, the other is across from the Hotel du Glacier-Sporting. Courts are open from 8 am to 10 pm. Inquire at the Tourist Office.
- Boating - row boats and pedal boats can be rented at the boat house on the lake.
- Fishing - trout fishing from June through October. Check with the Tourist Office for rules and permit rates.
- Excursions by Helicopter - Call Air-Glacier in Sion, 027/22-64-64 for information.
- Alpine Garden - situated above the village and north of the campsite. There are over 4,000 types of plants and flowers in their natural surroundings. Check with the Champex Tourist Office for exhibit hours. (See Walk #1.)

Excursions in and Around Champex

This section introduces day excursions for *Easy Walkers* to enjoy when the weather is not suitable for walking, or when an alternative to walking is desired. Be sure to check local timetables for best connections if using public transportation.

1. La Breya (Champex) - Télésiège Champex-La Breya is a two-stage chair lift, climbing near the summit of La Breya at 7,181 ft. From this ascent above Lake Champex, you can see the winding road from Orsières to Champex, and the foothills of the Mont Blanc range, sloping down into the nearby Ferret Valley. This high setting provides wonderful views of the Valaisian countryside. (See Walk #2.)

Directions to La Breya: Walk west on Champex's main street, away from the lake and up the hill. After 10 minutes, you'll see the chair lift on the the left. They run every 1/2 hour after 9 am.

2. Great Saint Bernard Pass and Hospice - Twenty-one miles southeast of Champex, the Hospice stands at the highest point (8,100 ft.) on the Great Saint Bernard Pass and Road, now by-passed by the new tunnel. On the edge of a lake frozen 265 days a year, the Hospice is the home of the grand, gentle dogs noted for carrying brandy kegs to travelers stranded in the mountain snows. The Chapel, with its pulpits and stalls dating from the 17th century, and the Museum's pictures and memorabilia, should be visited. The famous Grand Saint Bernard dogs, who accompanied the monks on their rescue missions, are in the kennels behind the hotel. Today, since helicopters have taken their place, the dogs sleep most of the day. (See Walk #6.)

There is a chairlift near the Hospice, one of the highest in the world. It can take you to La Chenalette at 9,476 ft., with a wondrous view of 27 glaciers.

Directions to Great Saint Bernard Hospice: Take the 9:00 am bus from Champex to Orsières, and change for the direct bus to the Hospice and the Pass. You'll arrive in St. Bernard at 10:30 am. To return, take the bus to Orsières and change for the bus to Champex.

3. Orsières - The small village of Orsières, with a population of 2,400, nestles at the junction of the Ferret and the Entremont Valleys. Before catching the bus to Champex, explore its charming streets. Across from the church is the well-tended, flower-bedecked, local cemetery where very clean public restrooms can be found. The hotel at the railroad station serves lunch, and the bake shop down from the station sells mouth-watering pastries.

Directions to Orsières: Every bus from Champex winds down the road into Orsières to the railroad station.

4. Sion - As you approach the train station in Sion, two rocky hills dominate the landscape. A ruined fortress (Tourbillon), is on one hill. On the other hill (Valère), stands a church containing the oldest playable organ in the world, built in 1390. Walk Sion's narrow, old streets and visit the Sorcerer's Tower, the 17th-century Town Hall with its magnificent carved doors and an astronomical clock. Many examples of Celtic, Roman and medieval art and artifacts can be found in the Cathedral of Notre Dame du Glarier. The views from the top of the two hills with their Disney-like ruins are excellent. The hills are reached by rather steep walking paths, but Valeria, with its castle, basilica, organ and museum, should be seen.

Directions to Sion: Take an early bus from Champex to Orsières, and change in Orsières for the train to Martigny. In Martigny, take the train east to Sion. To return to Champex, catch the train from Sion west to Martigny, where you change for the train to Orsières, and the bus to Champex.

5. Sierre - This town is in the heart of the wine district of the Valais region, and the local tourist office can supply you with maps for walks through the surrounding vineyards. Sierre is one of the sunniest and driest cities in Switzerland, with more than 200 days of sunshine and only 24 inches of rain per year. Walk on the Rue du Bourg and explore the "old quarter." Notice a 15th-century tower castle, a 12th-century monastery, a 13th-century tower house and the Gothic church of Notre Dame des Marais. Interesting note: in Sierre, the language changes from French to German.

Directions to Sierre: Take the early morning bus from Champex to Orsières, and change for the train to Martigny. In Martigny, take a train east to Sierre. To return, take a train from Sierre to Martigny and change for the train to Orsières, and the bus to Champex.

6. Verbier - This well-known ski resort lies northeast of Champex on a large, sunny plateau in the Bagnes Valley. At 5,000 ft.,the area around Verbier was meadowland before the town developed into the all-season resort it is today. Even when surrounding meadows are blooming with flowers, the nearby Combin and Mount Blanc mountains are covered with snow. The Haut Val de Bagnes Nature Reserve has hundreds of species of native plants.

Directions to Verbier: Take the early morning bus from Champex to Orsières and change for the train to Sembrancher. In Sembrancher, change for the train to Le Chable, where you can catch the PTT bus to Verbier, or take the Le Chable-Verbier aerial cableway. To return to Champex, take the bus or cable car from Verbier to Le Chable, the train to Sembrancher, and another train to Orsières, where you catch the bus to Champex.

7. Montreux - This beautiful town, sometimes called "The Vaud Riviera," is the most popular resort on Lac Léman (Lake Geneva)—noted for its mild weather producing a Mediter-ranean feeling in summer. Enjoy the path that runs for miles along the lake, planted with all types of semi-tropical plants and flowers—a wonderful contrast to the snowy scenery and wintery pine forests around Champex. The castle of Chillon, made famous by the poet Byron, is only 1 1/2 miles from Montreux. Check at the train station in Montreux for the schedule of buses to the castle. From the Montreux railroad station, *Easy Walkers* can also take an excursion by mountain railroad to Rochers de Naye, at 7,000 ft. It affords a marvelous view of the lake, ringed by the French and Swiss Alps, and there are pleasant paths winding through the countryside. Allow 1 hour each way for the train trip to Rochers de Naye.

Directions to Montreux: Take the early morning bus from Champex to Orsières, and change for the train to Martigny. In Martigny, change for the train to Montreux. To return to Cham-pex, take any train from Montreux to Martigny, change for the train to Orsières, and the bus to Champex.

8. Iserable - The ride from Riddes (9 miles east of Martigny) to Iserable, via cable car, is unforgettable. The cable car rises high above colorful meadows to a platform built of rock at the entrance of this tiny village. At 3,400 ft., Iserable consists of a single, small street, bordered with chalets and old barns, lead-ing to a Romanesque church. The well-preserved old barns or mazots are raised on stones to prevent rodents from eating the feed. It has been said that the the dark-skinned, dark-eyed inhabitants of Iserable are descended from the Saracens who conquered isolated alpine villages in the early 8th century.

Directions to Iserable: Take an early morning bus from Champex to Orsières, and change for the train to Martigny. In Martigny, take a local train east to Riddes. There is a cable car in Riddes, rising to Iserables. To return, take the cable car down to Riddes and catch a westbound train to Martigny, where you change for the train to Orsières. In Orsières, take the bus to Champex.

9. Lausanne - Lausanne's cathedral is reputedly the most beautiful Gothic building in Switzerland—its picturesque towers and sculptured doors dating from 1175 to 1275. The cathedral boasts one of the last "watches" in the world, whose duty it is to "cry the hours" from 10 pm to 2 am. Lausanne is home to the first museum in French-speaking Switzerland devoted solely to modern art. The FAE Museum of Contemporary Art is on the shore of Lake Geneva in Pully, about 10 minutes from the city center. Ouchy, a bustling port on Lake Geneva, is now the "lakefront" for Lausanne, originally built up and away from the lake. Ouchy's shady piers provide delightful views over the port, the lake and the mountains.

Directions to Lausanne: Take the bus from Champex to Orsières and change for the train to Martigny. In Martigny, take the train to Lausanne. To return, take the train from Lausanne to Martigny, and change for the train to Orsières. In Orsières change for the bus to Champex.

10. Chamonix, France - Chamonix, at 3,280 ft., is the most famous resort in the French Alps, with commanding views of Mount Blanc, the highest mountain in Europe. The téléphérique (cable car) ascent to the Aguille du Midi is an exciting ride to an icy world of high mountain vistas. If time permits, the train ride to the Mer de Glace (River of Ice) glacier is another memorable excursion. Both of these trips begin near the main train station—just follow the signs when disembarking. Remember, the top of the Aguille can be *very* cold—put those insulated jackets into your backpacks before leaving Champex.

Directions to Chamonix, France: Take the early bus from Champex to Orsières and change for the train to Martigny. In Martigny, take the train to Chamonix. **Remember your passport!**

Champex Walks

Walk #1: Champex to Champex - A Walk Around the Lake (including excursion to the Alpine Garden)

 Walking Time - 2 hours

A walk around Lake Champex is a good way to become acquainted with the lake and village of Champex. The Jardin Florealpe (Alpine Garden), with over 4,000 different specimens of flowers from every area of Switzerland, nestled on a low bluff overlooking the village and lake, will also be visited. The walk itself ascends easily to the Alpine Garden, and returns to the opposite end of Champex via a higher path, ending at the Hotel Splendide, aptly named because of its beautiful, panoramic views overlooking two adjacent valleys. You then follow an easy path around the quiet shores of the lake.

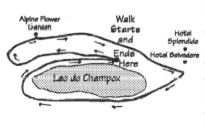

Start: Head west up the main street, towards the La Breya chairlift. Before reaching the chairlift, note a sign on the right reading "Jardin Florealpe." Turn right and walk past the campsite, turning right again on the Tour de Champex, a gently rising path through the woods and chalets. The lake and village are always a short distance below and to the right—rarely out of sight. When you reach the Jardin Florealpe, spend some time enjoying its great variety of native plants. As you leave the Alpine Garden, turn left and continue on the Tour de Champex along a path above and paralleling the lake. The trail begins to descend gently, with Champex and the lake visible on the right. You can reach the main, lakeside road by turning right at a junction with a path just below the Hotels Splendide and Belvédère, on the eastern end of town. Both of these hotels offer magnificent views into the St. Bernard and Ferret Valleys, where *Easy Walkers* will hike on other days. (See Walks #3 and #6.)

Continue the walk and turn right on the car road leading back to the lake. Turn left on the shore path, or "Tour du Lac," and follow it entirely around the lake. This path follows the banks of the small, glacial lake for most of the way, bringing you back into town at the "Au Club Alpin" restaurant. For a slightly longer variation, take the left fork "Chemin du Revers" trail at the Protestant Chapel. This path takes you into the woods around the lake and ends on the car road just before the La Breya chairlift. Turn right for the short walk into Champex.

This exploratory walk will give you the opportunity for a free afternoon in Champex. Enjoy lunch in an outdoor cafe, wander through the tiny town and its shops, pedal a boat on the lake, play tennis, swim in the heated pool, fish for trout (See Activities.), sit on the sun-terrace of the Belvédère or Splendide and drink in the view along with your coffee or beer, or just relax on the balcony of your hotel and enjoy tiny Lake Champex—hidden in its mountain aerie—a wonderful example of the French-speaking Valais region of Switzerland.

Walk #2: La Breya to Champex

   Walking Time - 2½ hours   

The summit of La Breya, at 7,181 ft., is a perfect spot to admire the turquoise beauty of Lake Champex, far below in the Drance Valley, surrounded by the Valais Alps. The La Breya chairlift will aid *Easy Walkers* in ascending this peak. Enjoy the panoramic view of Champex, its lake, mountains and glacial valleys before finding the trail down. A small snack shop and facilities are at the top.

Directions: After breakfast, pick up provisions for a picnic lunch. Walk west in Champex on the main street, up the hill and away from the lake, past the bakery, and you'll see the chairlift on the left. Buy a one-way Champex to La Breya ticket and take the 15-minute ride to the top. The Télésiège Champex-La Breya runs every hour on the hour, beginning at 9 am. Plan on taking the 10 am chairlift.

La Breya
7,179 ft.

Hotel
Belvédère

Lac de Champex
4,810 ft.

Hotel
Splendide

Hotel
du Glacier-Sporting

Walk Starts
and Ends Here

Start: Outside the chairlift station are two signs marked "Champex." Follow the sign straight ahead as you get off the cable car. After a few feet, another sign is marked in red lettering, "Champex - 2 hrs." This trail is very wide, but rocky—the trail will be more natural later in the walk. As you gradually descend, notice the open, panoramic views into an ancient, glacial valley—the Val d'Arpette—where you'll be hiking another day. (See Walk #4.)

After walking an hour, ignore a red arrow on your left on a small side trail. This trail leads to the Val d'Arpette. Continue on the wider, main trail, descending into the valley and the Arpette meadows. Cows with their typical Swiss leather collars and bells are grazing. Approaching two farmhouses, make sure you close the gate across the path so the cows don't go astray. Pause for a moment, turn, and look back for a breathtaking view of meadow, mountain and glacier.

Continue down the trail, passing a restaurant—where the path becomes a car road through the forest, all the way into Champex. Just beyond the restaurant is a challenging, alternative trail to Champex. It's marked "Champex - Sentier Ruisseau," or "path through the woods." If you decide to take this route, note a sign, "Champex d'en Bas Bovine." Follow this path, and turn right where it meets a wider path. The wide trail soon empties into a road. Turn right on the road, and walk into Champex, passing the La Breya Télésiège where this morning's walk began. As you pass the chairlift and parking lot on the right, notice a group of signs. Follow "Tour de Champex." The blue-blazed, descending trail is on a well-groomed path, crossing over a small stream and forking to the left, around the lake. Enjoy your picnic lunch on one of the many benches placed at scenic locations around the lake. Continue on this path as it circles Champex-Lac, bringing *Easy Walkers* back to town.

Walk #3: Champex to Issert to Praz de Fort to Issert to Orsières

 Walking Time - 4½ hours

Today's hike is a particularly beautiful and aggressive walk down to, and through the Val de Ferret (Ferret Valley). It is longer than most hikes, and we recommend that you begin by 9:30 am.

Start: Buy your picnic lunch provisions and walk on the car road as it begins to descend into Orsières, on the eastern end of Lake Champex (opposite direction from the La Breya chairlift). A yellow-signed trail marked "Prassurny" and "Val de Ferret," 6/10ths of a mile from the middle of town, is across from the sign welcoming you to Champex (as you come *up* the hill from Orsières). Taking this trail off the road and to the right, cross over a small stream, following the yellow-blazed path to the left—you are on the way to Issert. *Easy Walkers*: always follow the yellow-blazed trail in this area. The trail ascends, but you'll soon be walking downhill again. An interesting note—this trail is part of the "Tour de Mont Blanc," a famous hike in Europe. At the signs marked "Issert" and "Val de Ferret," proceed in the direction of Issert.

There are many offshoots of the main path, follow the yellow blazes. In about 20 minutes you may see a sign, "Champex - 20 min." The sign is for hikers walking *up* the mountain and is sometimes turned the wrong way! At a fork in the path, stay to the left on the main trail. At another fork, notice a door into the rocky mountain. This is probably the entrance into a Swiss Army fortification. Take the yellow-blazed, right-hand fork, go

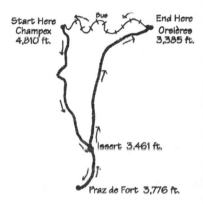

up a small incline, to another sign saying, "Champex - 30 min.," again for hikers walking *up* on the Tour de Mont Blanc. Continue to follow the yellow blazes and at yet another fork, bear left, staying on the main path. Proceed ahead as the trail begins to narrow and descend at a steeper rate, yellow blazes continuing to mark the way. After buttonhooking back and forth, the trail hits into an unsigned dead end. Turn left, pass a raised, wooden platform, and walk to a road. Make a right turn on the road, and turn right again, to walk onto private property with two homes. Walk between the two houses, and to the left, at the rear, will be the marked path continuing the descent to Issert. As you walk down, notice that the blazes in this section have changed to yellow and red. This path rises and falls for a short while, until you arrive at a sign marked "Issert." Take the left path, descending steeply toward Issert, with the trail still blazed yellow and red. At Sentiere Pedestre, the path forks. Walk to the left, following the yellow blazes and directions to "Issert." The path descends sharply, and suddenly Issert is ahead in the Ferret Valley. Turn right and follow the car road a short distance into town.

The sleepy village of Issert is made up of 70 to 80 houses and barns, some dating back to the 18th century. There is a PTT stop and a small restaurant in town. *Easy Walkers* now have an option of taking the bus to Orsières and changing for the bus to Champex, or continuing the hike to Les Arleches and Praz de Fort, charming little communities in the valley ahead.

If you decide to continue, walk along the main road, past the bus stop for a few hundred yards, and turn left at a yellow mailbox. Cross over the stream, and take a right turn onto the path to Les Arleches. The trail is yellow-blazed as you walk through the fields, with the stream on the right. This part of the walk, rolling through meadow and farmland, offers un-hampered views of the valley and its surrounding mountains. The road is sometimes bisected and trisected by other paths— stay on the lower, main path—going straight ahead along the river. In June and July, the fields are ablaze with color and the visual experience is remarkable. Late August and September brings a more autumnal feeling, with many of the flowers dried by the sun. *Easy Walkers*, please don't pick the flowers—most are protected by law. This well-marked path continues through the fields, but if you were to stop and look back, you'd see the Hotel Splendide, with its commanding view of two valleys, perched high on the side of the mountain.

It's a 15-minute walk from Issert to the even tinier hamlet of Les Arleches—a place where time seems to have stood still— a quiet village of a dozen buildings. The street through town is narrow, and the gray buildings on either side are brilliantly offset by multitudes of colorful flowers in their window baskets. Follow the yellow blazes through Les Arleches to Praz de Fort, walking through the Val de Ferret, with splendid views of the mountains on either side of the valley.

The small town of Praz de Fort comes into view after half an hour of walking from Les Arleches. As you enter the town, the bus stop is ahead of you, presenting *Easy Walkers* with another alternative return to Orsières and then Champex. If this is your decision, check the local bus schedule posted at the stop.

To continue, reverse direction and follow the same path back toward Issert. This gives hikers a different perspective of the valley, with the sun now behind you. When you reach the PTT bus stop in Issert, you can take advantage of your third option— returning now to Orsières by bus.

If you decide to walk the easy 2 1/2 miles into Orsières, turn right onto the main road. Pass through Som le Praz, a small suburb of Orsières, before arriving at the railroad station to catch the bus to Champex. It's important to remember that bus service to Champex is limited, with no service after 6:15 pm, so always carry a schedule with you. If you plan to catch the afternoon bus back to Champex, be prepared to line up early—this is a popular bus with returning school children and hikers.

Walk #4: Champex to Val d'Arpette to Champex

 Walking Time - 2½ hours

Easy Walkers will explore the Arpette meadow and valley, with the option to go forward and ascend near La Fenêtre d'-Arpette (the window of Arpette), and return to Champex through the same valley.

Start: Pick up lunch and walk up the road to the west, away from town. A large sign immediately before the La Breya chairlift points to "Val d'Arpette." Follow the major Val d'-Arpette sign, walking left and then right. This wide, dirt auto road ascends steeply through logging forests for 30 minutes, till you reach the hotel/restaurant "Relais d'Arpette." Cross over the proverbial babbling brook, walking through a wooden gate and closing it behind you so the cows in the meadow won't stray. The road becomes a path—follow it gradually upward

through the Arpette meadow, then over a rocky trail to the right to Val d'Arpette. Notice the steepening ascent—*turn back* whenever you feel the trail is uncomfortable for you. Remember that this walk began in Champex at 5,000 ft., and the trail rises to 8,700 ft. at the top of Fenêtre d'-Arpette—so we stress that you walk only as long as you

can *Walk Easy*. The route followed by this walk is one of the optional sections in the famous Tour de Mont Blanc, a long-distance hike from Chamonix, following well-marked paths from France into Switzerland, and returning by way of Italy and the Aosta Valley. The walk to Fenêtre d'Arpette is high-level excitement, taking you into a tiny corner of massive peaks and glaciers surrounding the Mont Blanc range. Awe-inspiring views of the upper Trient valley and the icy wilderness of the Trient Glacier are at the top of the pass.

We recommend walking until you feel satisfied with your accomplishment. On your return, a picnic lunch will taste ter-rific under a big tree in the Arpette meadow. To return to Cham-pex, retrace your steps and follow the path down the hill, ending near the bottom station of the La Breya chairlift. Turn right and follow the road into Champex.

Walk #5: Champex to Sembrancher

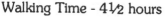

Walking Time - 4½ hours

Today's path will descend easily through forests and across meadows before reaching Sembrancher. *Easy Walkers* will pass through small farming hamlets high on the green hillsides, each with paths into the valley if you decide to cut your walk short because of weather or fatigue. The interesting, centuries-old architecture of the farmhouses and barns lend themselves to exploration and photography.

Start: Pick up a picnic lunch and walk east, down the main road in the direction of Orsières. When you get to the eastern end of the lake, veer left and walk on the road past the Belvédère Hotel till you reach the restaurant parking lot. At the side of the restaurant, take a path on the left and walk straight ahead,

gradually descending through the woods and coming out on the zigzag road to Orsières. Turn left, away from the road, and walk to a second bend. The trail borders the road and then ascends into the forest to the hamlet of Chez les Reuse. Continuing on this main path, follow it along the fields. Walk through a finger of forest, crossing a ravine. At the next intersection turn right, walking across the meadows above Verlona. Walk through Verlona and then two forested areas to a road leading to the even tinier— Sous la Lé. After walking through Sous la Lé, follow a path through the trees. Cross a small stream and ascend easily to La Garde. There is a road from La Garde to Sembrancher, but the trails are more interesting. We recommend bearing left through

La Garde. Following this path, walk down into the valley. Turn left, meeting a road, and turning left again. Follow this road, buttonhooking downhill, till you reach Sembrancher. Explore Sembrancher—an outdoor café is a good place to relax and observe the inhabitants of this busy little town.

To return to Champex, take the train from Sembrancher to Orsières and change for the Champex bus.

Walk #6: Excursion and Walk - Hospice at Great Saint Bernard Pass

Walking Time - 1-3 hours

The training area of the famous Grand Saint Bernard dogs is the focus of today's excursion. *Easy Walkers* will travel to the Great Saint Bernard Pass, linking Switzerland to Italy. For centuries this pass was closed for more than six months a year because of the winter snows. Now visitors can take the marvelously engineered new road into the 3 1/2 mile long St. Bernard Tunnel, enabling use of this important international route all year long. However, you will visit the 8,100 ft. Hospice, bypassed by the new tunnel, the highest point on the old road because its founder wanted to be sure it could be seen from a distance. For centuries, St. Bernard dogs helped priests find stranded travelers. Today, although helicopters have taken the place of the dogs, their romantic stories live on.

Directions: Backpack your picnic lunch and insulated jackets and take the 9:00 am bus from Champex to Orsières, changing for the bus to the St. Bernard Pass. The bus is painted with fabulous turn-of-the-century type pictures of dogs and priests. Sit on the right side of the bus (facing front) for the best views of the scenic mountains and valleys, although the lack of vegetation and trees becomes apparent from either side as the bus ascends. Notice the hikers and mountain climbers on the trails, as they wend their way to and from the Pass. It may

The trail from Planplatten, over the Balmeregghorn to Engstlenalp-Meiringen.

June in the Bernese Oberland-Lauterbrunnen Valley.

View of the 900 ft. Staubbach Falls - Lauterbrunnen Valley.

The glacier above Engelberg (Photo - Engelberg Tourist Office)

The path to Trummelbach Falls and Stechelberg - Lauterbrunnen Valley.

Swiss cows in full dress, celebrating their return to lower pastures from summer grazing in the alps.

View of the Matterhorn from the sun-terrace of the Hotel Riffelalp - Zermatt.

Easy Walkers taking the easy way up the mountains - Saas-Fee.

surprise you that just below the Hospice is the border between Switzerland and Italy. Although you will not travel to Aosta in Italy today, that area is distinctly Mediterranean in character—very different from the world where snow drifts reach 12 ft. in winter and the lake is frozen over 265 days a year!

Visit the museum at the Hospice. After paying a small fee, walk through a pictorial history of the pass, the Hospice and the Grand Saint Bernard dogs. This pass, called "Mount of Jupiter," was already a holy place in the Roman era, and the mementos of Napoleon and his crossing of the Alps certainly add interest to its story. The famous Grand St. Bernard dogs who accompanied the monks on their errands of mercy may be seen in the kennels behind the hotel. Twenty of the dogs are cared for and bred in order to maintain the traditional line.

Start: After the museum, choose some of the walk options in the area. There is an enjoyable walking trail overlooking the small lake and ending at the customs station in Italy—your passport is *not* needed to walk over the border. As you leave the museum, pick up the path above the road, on the right side. After a few minutes you'll see a sign annnouncing Italy! Continue maneuvering on a narrow, rocky, descending trail, allowing entrance to Italy, bypassing the customs station. Within a few minutes you'll be at the souvenir stands on the Italian side of the border. There are many paths in this area with grand views of Italy and Switzerland. Follow any of the trails and walk till you feel ready to return to the bus outside the Hospice, or return to the Hospice and follow any of the marked trails leading from the top.

Check the bus schedule for your return to Orsières, and Champex, before beginning any walk.

On The trail to Wengen   Bernese Oberland   ClutRupton

LAUTERBRUNNEN

Lauterbrunnen is in the Bernese Oberland, the heart of Switzerland, welcoming *Easy Walkers* with snow-capped peaks, grassy meadows, deep glacial valleys and spectacular waterfalls.

The tiny town of Lauterbrunnen nestles in one of those glacial valleys, and upon arrival you are captivated by a view of the hundreds of large and small waterfalls the town is named for. However, it is Staubbach Falls, dropping 1,000 ft. from the majestic Mürren cliff, that dominates the landscape, along with a panoramic view of the snow-covered Jungfrau and its neighboring mountains.

Most guidebooks pass over Lauterbrunnen, concentrating on Wengen and Mürren, car-free mountain villages that overlook the valley. However, Lauterbrunnen's location on the incomparable Swiss railroad system makes it the perfect place for trips almost anywhere in Switzerland. On any day, *Easy Walkers* can take the highest rack-railway in Europe to the sub-zero ice of the Jungfraujoch, and on the next day shop in the beautiful and cosmopolitan city of Lucerne.

The Lauterbrunnen Valley, surrounded by some of the world's finest trails, is a short train, bus or steamer ride away from access to *Walking Easy* at its best.

The incomparable beauty of this valley is nature's gift and, once experienced, will be with you forever.

Transportation

Zurich Airport to Lauterbrunnen - After claiming your baggage, buying Swiss francs at the Money Exchange window near the luggage carousels and clearing Swiss Customs, note the large sign marked "Bahnhof," with a symbol of a train. An agent at any ticket window will validate your Swiss Card or Swiss Pass. Take one of the frequent trains to Zurich Central and change for the train to Bern, checking the large, overhead information panels for the time and the track number. In Bern, change for the train to Interlaken Ost, where you take the train to Lauterbrunnen, on Track #2, leaving 31 minutes and 50 minutes past every hour. **Note: Sit in the front cars marked "Lauterbrunnen"—the back cars are marked "Grindelwald" and drop off in the town of Zweilütschinen for the trip to Grindelwald.**

If the transportation directions seem complicated, don't be concerned—it's really quite simple. There are several trains a day from Zurich that go directly to Interlaken Ost without a change in Bern. You might be able to board one at the main Zurich station, depending on the time your flight arrives. Don't hesitate to ask the railroad personnel for information—all speak English and are courteous and helpful. Remember, public transportation is the fastest and easiest way to see Switzerland.

If you are traveling to Lauterbrunnen from a point in Switzerland or Europe other than Zurich, please check local timetables. Remember, you must *always* change trains in Interlaken Ost for Lauterbrunnen.

Sample Timetable:

Zurich Airport to Zurich Central	**Take any train**
Zurich to Bern	**10:29 am dep.**
Bern	**12:09 pm arr.**
Bern to Interlaken Ost	**12:28 pm dep.**
Interlaken Ost	**13:21 pm arr.(1:21 pm)**
Interlaken Ost to Lauterbrunnen	**13:31 pm dep. (1:31 pm)**
Lauterbrunnen	**13:54 pm arr. (1:54 pm)**

Excursions in and Around Lauterbrunnen

This section introduces day excursions that *Easy Walkers* will enjoy when the weather is not suitable for high-altitude walking, or if an alternate activity is desired. Be sure to check local timetables for the best connections if public transportation is used. The Lauterbrunnen Tourist Office is on the main street, to the left of the small supermarket.

1. Grindelwald - This busy village lies at the foot of several imposing mountains, and in the shadow of the dark, north face of the Eiger. A tourist mecca famous for its shops as well as hiking trails, Grindelwald hosts many international tour groups, and boasts one of the busiest railroad stations in the Bernese Oberland. It serves as a central point for many low and high level walks, with three lifts offering access to sensational panoramic viewing, and used as the beginning of rewarding walks on other days.

    A. First - A new gondola has been installed from Grindelwald to First, replacing a multi-part chair lift, taking riders up another 3,000 ft. to panoramic views of the great Eiger north face, and the gloomy cliffs of the Wetterhorn, towering over tiny Grosse Scheidegg. First offers a restaurant, facilities, large sun-terrace, and is the starting point of many walks. (See Walk #4.)

    B. Pfingstegg - This cable car offers a host of rewarding views, and is located between Grindelwald's famous glaciers. Enjoy the view from Grosse Scheidegg to First. (See Walk #10.)

    C. Grindelwald-Männlichen Gondelbahn - At four miles in length, this is the longest gondola system in Europe. The entire trip from Grindelwald to Männlichen, or reverse, takes 30 minutes, with a 4,200 ft. rise in altitude. (See Walk #6.)

Directions to Grindelwald: Take the Interlaken Ost train from Lauterbrunnen to Zweilütschinen. In Zweilütschinen change for the train to Grindelwald. To return to Lauterbrunnen, take the Interlaken Ost train from Grindelwald to Zweilütschinen and change for the Lauterbrunnen train.

2. Interlaken - Interlaken, named for its location between Lake Thun and Lake Brienz, is a small, beautiful city, and a busy tourist center, surrounded by a superb mountain panorama. The "Höheweg," a wide street bustling with stores, restaurants and hotels, with trees and parks interspersed for pockets of quiet greenery, links the east (ost) section of Interlaken with the busy west area. Interlaken's casino (Kursaal), with its colorful gardens and large, floral clock, is on the Höheweg, past the splendid Hotel Victoria-Jungfrau. Lake steamer excursions can be enjoyed from Interlaken on the Thunersee or Brienzersee. The piers are only a minute's walk from either the Interlaken Ost or the Interlaken West train stations.

    A. Heimwehfluh - A 5-minute walk from the Interlaken West station brings *Easy Walkers* to the Heimwehfluh funicular railway, featuring an elaborate scale-model railroad, appealing to hobbyists from all over the world.

    B. Harder Kulm - Where it may still be possible to catch a glimpse of the rarely seen ibex at the top, is reached by a 15-minute funicular ride, a few minute's walk from the Interlaken Ost station. There are several well-marked trails at the top—one is an easy hour's walk around the summit. A restaurant, facilities and a large sun-terrace are at the peak.

    Directions to Interlaken: Take the train from Lauterbrunnen to Interlaken Ost and change for Interlaken West, in order to arrive at the main shopping area. When returning to Lauterbrunnen, reverse the procedure. An alternate return would be to walk from Interlaken West along the main shopping street, passing the Victoria Jungfrau Hotel and the casino, to reach the Interlaken Ost station—a 20-minute walk.

3. Mürren - A tiny, car-free hamlet of 350 people, Mürren is located on a sheltered, sunny terrace above the Lauterbrunnen Valley, and at 5,400 ft., is the highest village in the Bernese Oberland. It has incomparable views of the mountains—on a clear day it seems as though you can reach out and touch the Jungfrau. Mürren can be enjoyed for its charming hotels, chalets, and shops, as well as for its incredible scenery and miles of hiking trails. (See Walk #1.) A trip to Mürren can be combined easily with an excursion to the Schilthorn. (See Excursion #4.)

Directions to Mürren: Mürren is reached by a cable car from Stechelberg, or by funicular and rail from Lauterbrunnen.

4. Schilthorn - A cable car quietly ascends to 9,750 ft. to an incredible, ice-filled panorama. The Piz Gloria restaurant, made famous in the James Bond movie, *On Her Majesty's Secret Service*, revolves continuously and is justly renowned for its 360 degree view from Lake Geneva to Lake Constance. *Easy Walkers* should remember to dress warmly because temperatures can be below freezing! This trip to the top of the world can be combined with walks and an excursion to Mürren. (See Walk #1 and Excursion #3.)

Directions to the Schilthorn:

Alternate #1: From Lauterbrunnen station take the funicular to Grütschalp and change for the train to Mürren. In Mürren, walk through town to the Schilthorn lift station.

Alternate #2: From Lauterbrunnen station take the bus to Schilthornbahn, before the town of Stechelberg. The cable ascent to the Schilthorn is in four easy stages—stopping in Gimmelwald, Mürren and Birg, before reaching the top.

Alternate #3: Walk from Lauterbrunnen to the Schilthornbahn and take the cable car to the Schilthorn. (See Walk #1.)

5. Wengen - Situated on a sunny, protected ledge at 4,200 ft., overlooking the Lauterbrunnen Valley, Wengen is surrounded by high, snow-covered peaks of the Bernese Oberland. *Easy Walkers* will find it a perfect place to enjoy an outdoor lunch after a morning spent on the Jungfraujoch. (See Excursion #6.) Instead of returning to Lauterbrunnen by train, why not cap a wonderful day by walking down a forest trail with spectacular views of the Lauterbrunnen Valley and its waterfalls.

Although this path is wide and comfortable, the angle of descent steepens a bit. Look for the yellow sign in Wengen marked "Lauterbrunnen," and in 1 1/2 hours, *Easy Walkers* will be at their hotel.

Directions to Wengen: Trains from Lauterbrunnen to Wengen run frequently, and the scenic ride takes about 20 minutes.

6. Jungfraujoch -   The top of Europe is reached by the highest railway on the continent, above the clouds, climbing to an ice wonder-world at 11,723 ft. *Easy Walkers* must remember to dress **warmly** and move **slowly** on leaving the train.

From your change of train in Kleine Scheidegg, the next 4 1/2 mile rail trip is through a tunnel inside the Eiger and Mönch mountains, which took 16 years to build! At the intermediate stops of Eigerwand and Eismeer, windows have been cut into the face of the mountain, and as you look out, the magic world of ice and snow begins to reveal itself. At the top station there is a restaurant and gift shop—don't miss the "Ice Palace" with its intricate, permanent ice carvings. For an additional thrill, take the 5-minute ride in sleighs pulled by trained huskies. Upon returning from the Jungfraujoch, Wengen is a good place to stop for lunch, sightseeing and perhaps a walk down a winding forest trail to Lauterbrunnen. (See Excursion #5.)

Directions to the Jungfraujoch: Take the train from Lauterbrunnen to Kleine Scheidegg, via Wengen. Change in Kleine Scheidegg for the Jungfraujoch train. To return to Lauterbrunnen, reverse the procedure.

7. Schynige Platte -   At 6,500 ft., the Schynige Platte's marvelous panorama overlooks both mountains and lakes from Grindelwald to Interlaken. The famous old Schynige Platte Cog Railway is used for the trip up to this scenic plateau and its alpine garden.

At the top of Schynige Platte, a yellow sign directs you towards "Daube," where a short and vigorous uphill walk will whet your appetite. If you haven't brought a picnic lunch, the restaurant offers simple fare with an anything but simple view. Enjoy the panorama of the most famous mountains in the Bernese Oberland before catching the return train.

Directions to Schynige Platte: Take the train in Lauterbrunnen to Wilderswil and change for the 1-hour trip on the charming wooden trains with the red and white striped awnings. To return, take the train from the Schynige Platte to Wilderswil, and change for the Lauterbrunnen train.

8. Trümmelbach Falls - This spectacular, hidden wonder of nature cascades into the heart of the Lauterbrunnen Valley. A walk to the Falls from your hotel is a fine introduction to the beauty of this area. The ten, glacier-fed waterfalls inside a mountain, have been made accessible by a Swiss engineering miracle. It's cold and damp inside the mountain, so dress warmly.

Directions to Trümmelbach Falls: Walk through Lauterbrunnen on its main street, away from the railroad station. At the end of town, note a group of signs for cars and another group of yellow signs for walkers. Take the wide paved path towards "Trümmelbachfälle," passing the magnificent Staubbach Falls on the right. (See Walk #1.)

9. Brienz - Interested in woodcarving or violin-making? Be sure to visit Brienz, where you'll enjoy shopping in the many stores offering local artisans' work. You can combine this trip to Brienz with a visit to the 7,710 ft. Rothorn, on the only surviving steam-driven cog railroad in Switzerland. It takes one hour for the ride, with magnificent views of the countryside. The Brienz-Rothorn Bahn is open from June to late October, and steam-operated trains are numbered "5" and "7." Departures and arrivals are timed to the arrival of the Interlaken trains—passengers can hop off one train and on to the other. There are 9 scheduled round trips daily, but trains are added and dropped according to demand. Call ahead at 036 51 1232 for information. Another alternative when visiting Brienz is a visit to the Swiss Open Air Museum for an easy-to-take history of Switzerland's many cultures and styles of living. (See Excursion #10.)

Directions to Brienz: Take the train from Lauterbrunnen to Interlaken Ost and change for the train to Brienz. An alternate means of transportation to or from Interlaken Ost is by steamer. The dock in both Interlaken Ost and Brienz is outside the railroad station.

10. Swiss Open-Air Museum in Ballenberg -   This beautifully landscaped area provides fascinating insights into Swiss lifestyles of the past. It is a perfect way for *Easy Walkers* to painlessly learn about Swiss culture. All of Switzerland's cantons are represented in old, traditional buildings, and the crafts of another era are graphically depicted against a picture-perfect background of forests and mountains. Leave about 3 hours to explore the 7 separate areas, all connected by roads. When buying your admission ticket, ask for a map.

Directions to Ballenberg: Take the train from Lauterbrunnen to Interlaken Ost, changing for the train to Brienz and the bus to Ballenberg. To return, take the bus to Brienz and either the boat or train to Interlaken Ost changing for the train to Lauterbrunnen.

11. Thun - At the northern end of the Thunersee (Lake Thun), lies the medieval city of Thun, with its famous castle and picturesque streets. The town of Thun is also the center for a number of walks around the lake *Easy Walkers* might enjoy after exploring the old town and its castle. (See Walk #8.) Check with the tourist bureau in the Thun railroad station for a sightseeing map of Thun.

Directions to Thun: This fascinating city can be reached by taking the train from Lauterbrunnen to Interlaken Ost, then changing for the train to Thun. To return, take the train to Interlaken Ost and change for the Lauterbrunnen train.

12. Bern - The capital of Switzerland is a delightful city of medieval arches, fountains, towers, an ancient clock tower and, of course, the famous bear pits the city is named after. *Easy Walkers* will enjoy shopping and sightseeing in this typically Swiss city with a small-town feeling.

The Bern Tourist Office is located in the railroad station. They can supply you with city maps and additional sightseeing suggestions.

Directions to Bern: Take the train from Lauterbrunnen to Interlaken Ost and change for the train to Bern—an easy 1 1/2 hour trip. To return to Lauterbrunnen, take the train from Bern to Interlaken Ost and change for the Lauterbrunnen train.

13. Lucerne - This old, charming city is beautifully situated at the northwest end of Lake Lucerne. Still preserved are Lucerne's covered wooden bridges and the remains of the town's fortifications. Once a simple fishing village, Lucerne is now a fashion mecca for shoppers, and sightseers throng its narrow, cobblestone streets lined with painted houses. No trip to Lucerne is complete without a visit to the famous Lion Monument (Löwendenkmal)—a Lucerne trademark.

Directions to Lucerne: Take the train from Lauterbrunnen to Interlaken Ost and change for the train to Lucerne, a ride of about 1 3/4 hours. To return, take the train from Lucerne to Interlaken Ost and change for the Lauterbrunnen train.

14. Beatenberg/Niederhorn - Today, *Easy Walkers* will utilize every form of Swiss public transportation. To begin, take the train from Lauterbrunnen to Interlaken Ost and change for the train to Interlaken West (a short three-minute ride). Catch the Post Bus to Beatenberg outside the Interlaken West station. Enjoy the scenery along this winding road and ask the driver to let you out at the Beatenburg lift station. Take the 2-person chair lift to the 6,400 ft. summit of the Niederhorn. The panoramic views reach from the Bernese Oberland to Mont Blanc in France. For our avid *Easy Walkers*, there are many short hikes at the top—just pick a trail and walk till you are ready to return—enjoying the scenery without buildings or forests to obscure the views. After descending on the chairlift, take the bus for a short ride to the funicular down to Beatenbucht, and board the steamer to Interlaken West. You can enjoy lunch, shopping and sightseeing in Interlaken before walking to Interlaken Ost to catch the train to Lauterbrunnen. (See Excursion #2.)

Lauterbrunnen Walks

Walk #1: Lauterbrunnen to Stechelberg - and Mürren to Grütschalp (excursion to the Schilthorn)

Walking Time - 2 1/2 hours

This particularly rewarding walk will allow *Easy Walkers* to become acquainted with the lovely Lauterbrunnen Valley on an almost level path, past Staubbach Falls, Trummelbach Falls and the rapidly running Lütschine River. At Stechelberg you'll take the cable car to Gimmelwald and Mürren, and if the weather is clear, to the top of the Schilthorn. (See Excursions #3 and #4.) After enjoying the panorama from the Schilthorn, return to Mürren and continue on the last part of this walk from Mürren to Grütschalp, where you'll catch the 100 year-old funicular to Lauterbrunnen. Put a warm jacket in your backpack along with lunch. The Schilthorn is at 9,744 ft., and it can be quite cold.

Start: Walk south, away from the Lauterbrunnen station and up the hill towards the stores in town. Pick up a picnic lunch and pass through town, walking toward Staubbach Falls on the right. Follow a yellow-signed, paved path straight ahead to

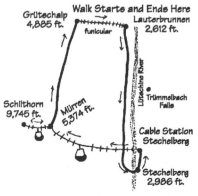

"Stechelberg - 1 hr., 15 min." As you proceed, the well-tended Lauterbrunnen cemetery is on the left, followed by the Jungfrau campsite. This walk parallels the Lütschine River, and in early summer the surrounding fields are ablaze with wild flowers—a perfect foil to the snow-capped mountains above. In autumn, the bright colors of the spring and summer flowers will be replaced by the subtler hues of the dried pods. However, flower gardens are in bloom till the first frost, and always provide the brilliant color photographers relish. Cows, goats and sheep dot the Lauterbrunnen Valley meadows, and there are many old barns filled with hay. The path is level and well-signed, so walk at your leisure—delight in the beauty of this glacial valley.

At the tiny hamlet of Buchen, a bridge crosses the river for a short walk to Trummelbach Falls. (See Excursion #8.) Today however, continue ahead on the main path. The Lütschine River turns closer to the trail and you'll soon arrive at a small bridge leading to the lift station. It's possible to cross the bridge and go directly to the Schilthorn lift, but we recommend continuing on the path another 15 minutes into Stechelberg. This is a lovely walk through the cool forest, along the swiftly flowing river. Follow the sign to "Stechelberg Post," into the center of town. At the post office, turn left on the paved auto road and walk 10 minutes back to the Schilthorn lift station. Buy a ticket, Stechelberg to Schilthorn, with return to Mürren only.

This large cable car runs frequently, and after changes in Gimmelwald and Mürren, you are brought up to Piz Gloria of James Bond fame. The views are incomparable from the top of the Schilthorn. The authors were there in the middle of June, and everything was covered with snow and ice. We were very glad to have put insulated jackets in our backpacks!

Take the cable car down to Mürren and spend some time in this tiny town with its grand views. Mürren is car-free and perched on a sunny hillside high above the Lauterbrunnen Valley. As you walk through town, many picnic opportunities are available— lunch can be a wondrous experience while overlooking the unfolding panorama.

After exploring Mürren, continue the walk to Grütschalp. A sign indicates "Grütschalp - 1 hr.," as the trail proceeds next to the railroad tracks. After a few minutes, this paved road becomes a dirt path. Don't be tempted by the signs pointing directly to Lauterbrunnen—these paths are usually steep and should be avoided by *Easy Walkers*. We can't praise the beauty of this path to Grütschalp too highly, as the trail wanders through pine forests and hillside pastures. You'll encounter friendly cows, sheep and goats, and the typically alpine sound of their echoing bells is a wonderful accompaniment to the spectacular mountain scenery. Wengen, on the other side of the Lauterbrunnen Valley, sits on a sunny plateau, with winding paths to be taken by *Easy Walkers* on other days. (See Walk #2.)

After walking 30 minutes to Winteregg, a restaurant with a spacious sun-terrace can be seen on the right. Enjoy the view, the grazing cows, perhaps some dessert, and follow the sign to the Grütschalp station. You'll be walking on a trail that is well-graded, well-maintained, and offers an impressive view of the Lauterbrunnen Valley. At the Grütschalp funicular station, buy a ticket for the return to Lauterbrunnen station.

Walk #2: Männlichen to Kleine Scheidegg to Wengernalp to Wengen

Walking Time - 3 1/2 hours

Easy Walkers will always treasure the memory of this walk and it is one of the authors' favorites. It should be taken on a reasonably clear day because the Männlichen panorama is unique in its loveliness, with unforgettable hiking routes and mountain views. The hike will begin in the shadow of many of Switzerland's most famous mountains—including the Eiger, the Mönch and the Jungfrau—and you'll walk on paths that furnish a view from the Grindelwald Valley to the Lauterbrunnen Valley.

Directions: Buy a one-way ticket, Lauterbrunnen to Männlichen (the lift ticket is included), and take the train from Lauterbrunnen to Wengen—a scenic 20-minute train ride. The Wengen-Männlichen cableway is only a short walk through town. Follow the yellow and green signs on the main shopping street, where provisions for a picnic lunch can be picked up if you didn't have time earlier. Board the large cable car for the quick ascent to the Männlichen station. This plateau is at 7,500 ft., and is a comfortable altitude for walkers of all ages. It's an interesting stop because the area offers many options, such as the 4-mile Grindelwald-Männlichen gondola cableway, the longest in Europe. But we'll hold that for a *Walking Easy* excursion. (See Excursion #1.)

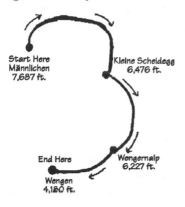

Start Here
Männlichen
7,687 ft.

Kleine Scheidegg
6,476 ft.

End Here

Wengernalp
6,227 ft.

Wengen
4,180 ft.

The Männlichen restaurant and its facilities are available, and after enjoying the panorama, proceed with today's walk.

Start: Begin at the Wengen-Männlichen cable car station and walk south, following the yellow sign marked "Kleine Scheidegg - 1 hr., 20 min." This wide path contours around a rocky mass of mountain. As you walk under the Grindelwald-Männlichen cable cars in the direction of the Eiger, used by Trevanian for the setting of his book, *The Eiger Sanction*, you are hiking just above the tree line on one of the most traveled paths in the Bernese Oberland. This well-signed walk has continuous views of the area's mountains: the Eiger, the Mönch and the Jungfrau dominate the landscape. Grindelwald will be on the left in the distant valley, as you walk easily down toward Kleine Scheidegg.

About 10 minutes before reaching Kleine Scheidegg, a walk through alpine pastures and beneath the Lauberhorn, brings you to the Grindelwaldblick restaurant, perched on a high point, with a singular view of the famous north wall of the Eiger. Climb to the top of a nearby lookout tower for an even better view of the unfolding mountain panorama. The Kleine Scheidegg station and hotel is just below, and after a short walk you'll reach this busy railroad stop—bustling with hikers, climbers and tourists changing for the train to and from the Jungfraujoch. (See Excursion #6.)

At Kleine Scheidegg, you have the option of taking the train back to Lauterbrunnen, but we suggest continuing with the walk to Wengernalp and Wengen.

Cross the railroad tracks at Kleine Scheidegg to find a sign directing you to "Wengernalp," on a path to the right. Wengernalp is the next stop on the train. It is an easy, 30-minute walk from Kleine Scheidegg on a wide, comfortable, well-signed trail. You are walking with the railroad tracks on your right, and the graceful peak of the Jungfrau on your left.

Could there be a more perfect spot to have your picnic than at the foot of the mountains at the top of the world? Benches are strategically placed for maximum scenic viewing.

Continuing this walk, the train will pass on your right, and a friendly wave will usually be returned with smiles and picture-taking from the passengers. You'll reach the Wengernalp station in 30 minutes. Walk in back of the small station and continue the trip to Wengen, following the yellow signs that point to the shortest and most direct route. This part of the path is in the open, with some high-level farms in the meadows, but as the treeline develops more fully, pine forests begin to appear. Follow the signed, well-defined path to Wengen, eventually passing under a small ski lift. Within an hour you'll reach the station at Allmend, with a charming outdoor restaurant directly on the path. Some hot tea and delicious homemade apple kuchen might be appealing now. Follow the paved path to Wengen and in 15 minutes the railroad station in Wengen is in sight. Wengen's picturesque chalets, old-world hotels and well-stocked shops are delightful to visit. (See Excursion #5.)

After this 3 1/2-hour hike, *Easy Walkers* can continue by following the yellow sign marked "Lauterbrunnen." This walk will take another 1 1/2 hours, and please be aware that although the path is wide, the angle of descent steepens a bit and you might want to save this walk for another day. (See Excursons #5 and #6.) Our recommendation—explore Wengen and take the train back to Lauterbrunnen.

Walk #3:   Iseltwald to Giessbach

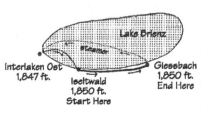

Walking Time - 1 3/4 hours

This lovely, low-altitude lake walk offers a wonderful change of pace for *Easy Walkers*. You will take a train to Interlaken Ost and a steamer on Lake Brienz to Iseltwald. This may be your only opportunity to use this wonderful form of Swiss transportation. A steamer ride provides a tranquil time to observe the alpine scenery from a very different vantage point. The walk will begin in Iseltwald and end in Giessbach, with a return to Interlaken Ost by the second steamer ride of the day. The afternoon can be free for shopping in Interlaken, or might include a trip by funicular to the Harder Kulm, an interesting mountain experience with another perspective of the Bernese Oberland. (See Excursion #2.)

Directions: After packing picnic provisions in Lauterbrunnen, buy a round-trip ticket, Lauterbrunnen to Interlaken, and board the train to Interlaken Ost. Upon leaving the train in Interlaken Ost and descending the platform steps, look for a large sign marked "Brienzersee," with a symbol of a ship. The pier is only a few minutes away—buy a ticket from Interlaken to Iseltwald with a return from Giessbach. *Easy Walkers* will enjoy a serene 45-minute boat ride on the lovely, unspoiled Brienzersee, to the tiny fishing village of Iseltwald. There are still fishermen working here, and they supply local restaurants with fresh fish. If you arrive in Iseltwald in the morning, look for the fishermen cleaning their catch, surrounded by ever-present birds waiting for their break-fast of fish scraps.

Start: When leaving the steamer, walk straight ahead where signs direct you to "Giessbach." Walking through the village, you'll soon be on a forest path with the lake on the left. This is a well-used trail, and hikers of all ages will be walking in both directions. In less than 1 1/2 hours, a sign points out an alternate route to Giessbach, up a mountain path to the Hotel Giessbach. Do not take this uphill trail but stay on the main path to "Giessbach" and "Brienz." Follow the next sign to "Giessbachsee," taking you left, through a small tunnel, to the steamer pier. Giessbach is only a steamer stop—made famous by the old, Victorian hotel on the mountain, and a nearby, un-usual, stepped waterfall. From the pier, take the funicular up to the hotel and waterfall. This is a quaint, old transportation sys-tem, in existence since 1879, the second oldest funicular rail-way in Switzerland. Make sure you check the posted steamer schedule before taking the funicular.

You can enjoy a picnic lunch near the waterfall, on the benches thoughtfully provided next to the pier, or by waiting until the steamer arrives and eating an alfresco lunch on the steamer deck. From Interlaken Ost it's only a 20-minute walk down the Höheweg to the main shopping area, or a 5-minute walk to the Harder Kulm funicular. (See Excursion #2.)

Sample Timetable:

Lauterbrunnen	**8:55 am dep.**
Interlaken Ost	**9:20 am arr.**
Interlaken Ost	**9:34 am dep. (steamship)**
Iseltwald	**10:16 am arr**
Giessbach	**1:55 pm dep. (steamship)**
Interlaken Ost	**2:20 pm arr.**

Walk #4:   First to Grosse Scheidegg
(including excursion to Grindelwald)

Walking Time - 2 1/2 hours

This walk is particularly interesting because it includes a visit to the famous town of Grindelwald, and a walk on its surrounding mountains. You will use train, bus and the First gondola, which takes *Easy Walkers* from bustling Grindelwald to peaceful alpine meadows, well above the tree line. This walk has excellent views of the Wetterhorn, whose dark cliffs seem to rise directly above Grosse Scheidegg. *Easy Walkers* will find today's trail totally open to views of the mountain ranges surrounding Grindelwald and Grosse Scheidegg. There will be time to visit Grindelwald before returning to Lauterbrunnen. (See Excursion #1.)

Directions: Pack a picnic lunch and buy a round-trip, Lauterbrunnen to Grindelwald ticket, via Zweilütschinen. Take the train from Lauterbrunnen to Zweilütschinen and change for the

train to Grindelwald, a very busy, tourist-filled town, but surrounded by many wonderful walks. Follow the signs through town to the First station, and buy a one-way ticket to the top.

Start: When you are ready to begin walking, walk out of the First sun-terrace and follow the sign to "Grosse Scheidegg - 1 1/2 hrs." This trail is entirely in the open, with nothing to block the magnificent view. Shortly, you'll see a yellow sign directing you straight ahead and slightly up to the left on the "Panoramaweg." This "Panoramaweg" becomes a nicely defined trail going around the upper part of the moun-

n. Follow its ascents and descents at a comfortable pace, noticing a group of alpine farms on a lower path—the small community of Grindel-Oberlager. The cows and their bells dominate the landscape here. This path, continuing in the shadow of the Schwarzhorn, crosses many streams, and eventually brings you directly into Grosse Scheidegg, and a restaurant with a reputation for good Swiss food, guarded by a sleepy Grand St. Bernard dog.

Check the posted bus schedule outside the restaurant for the return bus to Grindelwald. The ride, on a steep, narrow, winding road, offers incredible views of the valley, mountains and glaciers. It's an appropriate ending to a day of magnificent walking. Take some time to browse in Grindelwald and its many shops before your return to Lauterbrunnen.

Sample Timetable:

Lauterbrunnen	**9:08 am dep.**
Zweilütschinen	**9:18 am arr.**
Zweilütschinen	**9:46 am dep.**
Grindelwald	**10:09 am arr.**
Cable Car to First	**about 10:30 am**
Grosse Scheidegg	**2:40 pm dep. (bus)**
Grindelwald	**3:10 pm arr.**
Grindelwald	**4:48 pm dep.**
Zweilütschinen	**5:13 pm arr.**
Zweilütschinen	**5:45 pm dep.**
Lauterbrunnen	**5:54 pm arr.**

Walk #5:   Grütschalp to Isenfluh to Lauterbrunnen (including excursion to Sulwald)

 Walking Time - 2 1/2 hours

Today's outing takes *Easy Walkers* by funicular to Grütschalp, a car-free town accessible only by cable car or on foot, on the heights above the Lauterbrunnen Valley. The walk will begin at the Grütschalp station, winding through the forest to Isenfluh. This charming little town offers a chairlift to the Sulwald, a wonderful meadow with panoramic views of Grindelwald and Schynige Platte. After returning to Isenfluh, the walk will continue back to Lauterbrunnen by a lower path.

Directions: An early start is not necessary today, so if you've picked up your picnic lunch and arrived at the funicular across from the Lauterbrunnen railroad station by 10 am, you should be back at your hotel by 4 pm. Purchase a one-way funicular ticket to Grütschalp.

Start: Arriving at the top, don't take the waiting train going on to Mürren. Walk aross the tracks in front of the train

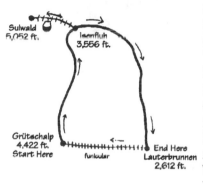

to a sign sending you to the right, to Isenfluh. One sign says "Isenfluh - 3 hrs.," and another sign indicates "Isenfluh - 1 hr., 10 min." Follow this latter sign to the right, to a second sign directing you down the hill. This descending, grassy path is occasionally blazed in yellow. The path zigzags, and soon you'll see Wengen, across the Lauterbrunnen Valley. To the right of Wengen is the graceful, snow-covered peak of the Jungfrau. The blazed path continues at a comfortable rate of descent. Within 15 or 20 minutes, you'll reach the Grütschalp funicular tracks, where the trail turns sharply to the left and continues downhill. This is a particularly pretty forest path, under tall pine trees, with views of Wengen and the Lauterbrunnen Valley. Proceed gently down the mountain with the friendly yellow diamond blazes indicating the correct "Wanderweg" path to Isenfluh. This forest trail eventually joins a wide, gravel path. Turn left and continue uphill, past a sign indicating "Isenfluh - 40 min." After crossing several cascading waterfalls, the road divides, one path continuing up the hill toward the left, the other path moving downhill to the right. This division may not be marked, but *Easy Walkers* should take the descending road to the right, leading to Isenfluh, which you approach within a short time. Take a small, local, fenced path on your right and walk to the small lift station taking you to the Sulwald meadow, above Isenfluh.

The station is unattended, but a sign clearly indicating operating times is posted. Ring the bell, and in a few minutes someone will arrive to send you up in the cable car to the grassy Sulwald meadow. This alpine meadow is a very special place—enjoy! Upon returning to Isenfluh, continue down the little path in front of the station to a sign, "Lauterbrunnen - 50 min.," indicating the paved path to the right. As you proceed, pass under another lift which originates on the main road outside of Lauterbrunnen—an alternative means of reaching Isenfluh. At this point you have the option of taking this cable car directly down to the Lauterbrunnen road, crossing over the little bridge on the Lütschine River, turning right, and walking along the river on a path which will take you to Lauterbrunnen in about half an hour.

Instead of the cable car descent, we suggest you choose the comfortable road down to Lauterbrunnen, about 1 hour of *Easy Walking* through the forest. At the end of the walk, the road goes under the Lauterbrunnen-Grütschalp funicular—the road taking you directly in front of the Hotel Silberhorn.

Walk #6: Männlichen to Grindelwald

 Walking Time - 4 1/2 hours

Today's walk brings you to Wengen by train and to Männlichen by cable car. The downhill walk to Grindelwald through alpine meadows and pine forests is in the shadows of the great mountain peaks overlooking the Grindelwald valley.

Directions: Pick up provisions for a picnic lunch and buy a ticket from Lauterbrunnen to Männlichen. Take the scenic,

20-minute train ride up to Wengen and follow the green and yellow signs through Wengen to the Männlichen Cable Station. Board the cable car for the quick ride to Männlichen, at 7,200 ft., where a restaurant and facilities are available.

Start: As you leave the gondola station, take the path marked "Grindelwald - 3 hrs., 10 min." We feel however, that *Easy Walkers* will need 4 1/2 hours to complete the walk to Grindelwald station. This is downhill all the way—through the meadows and cow pastures, surrounded by mountains. The initial part of this path is on a paved, descending road, under the Grindelwald-Männlichen gondolas, one of the longest cable car systems in Europe. The north face of the Eiger is in full view for most of this trip. The path is blazed in red and white, and a red and white marker takes you from the paved path to a grassy path across a meadow and to the right. At this point, the cable car is on the left. Within a short time you'll notice trees on both sides of the

pastures, as the tree line develops. If you are walking this trail in June and July, wild flowers will be ablaze and the waves of color will astound you. If your walk takes place in September, these same flowers are now dried and windblown, and have the more subdued tints of autumn. As you proceed, the Eiger, the Mönch and the Jungfrau are fully visible on the right, with the Schreckhorn and the Wetterhorn to your front right. Grindelwald is always in front of you, becoming more visible as you walk.

The walk crisscrosses the paved path, but follow the red and white blazes as they continue off the paved road and back on to a meadow trail. Every so often you'll pass through a gate which should be closed to keep the cows from straying. Since you are walking through pasture you might be cautious about where you step—the cows graze throughout the meadow.

Continue to follow the signs and blazes to Grindelwald, and Holenstein, the middle station on the Grindelwald-Männlichen cable car. In 1 1/2 hours you've walked down 2,000 ft. on an easy, scenic meadow path. At the middle station there are several benches with superb views of the mountains and the Grindelwald valley—a great spot for *Easy Walkers* to stop and picnic.

You have the option of proceeding down to Grindelwald by cable car, or continuing the walk to Grindelwald—about 3 hours more. To continue walking, at Holenstein, follow the yellow signs to the right to "Grindelwald Grund" and "Grindelwald Dorf." This path proceeds downhill at a steeper angle of descent and is now yellow-blazed. In about 10 minutes a paved road appears. Turn left and in a minute there will be another paved road. Facing you, on a barn in a small cow pasture, is a yellow, "Grindelwald-Wanderweg" sign. Cross the road, into the pasture, and follow this "Wanderweg" path to the right, and on to a forest path. This path also goes onto the paved road for short stretches, but pick up the "Wanderweg" sign and trail each time. As you get closer to Grindelwald, yellow signs indicate the way to Grindelwald Dorf and the railroad station. If you prefer not to walk up the hill to the main railroad station, walk to Grindelwald Grund and wait for a train or bus. They run every half-hour from Grindelwald Grund to Grindelwald Dorf.

Walk #7:   Lauterbrunnen to Zweilütschinen to Wilderswil to Interlaken (excursion to Interlaken)

 Walking Time - 3 1/2 hours

Today's walk can be reserved for a day when low clouds or drizzle are not conducive to high altitude exploration. This walk will take you from the Lauterbrunnen railroad station all the way to Interlaken, passing through the charming towns of

Zweilütschinen, Gsteigwiler and Wilderswil, and to the city of Interlaken for shopping and sightseeing. (*See Excursion #2.*)

The appeal of this low level walk is that it can be shortened or extended, at each railroad station. *Easy Walking* does not have to be abandoned if the weather does not cooperate.

This walk follows along the river as far as Zweilütschinen, where the Schwarz Lütschine and Weisse Lütschine merge, and

flow as one river through Wilderswil and down to the Brienzersee. After crossing the river in Zweilütschinen (two Lütschines), the path gradually veers away from the river bank and winds through the forest to Gsteigwiler, where it passes through the village and gradually descends through meadow and woods to Wilderswil, and on to Interlaken.

Start: After you've packed your picnic lunch, begin this walk at the Lauterbrunnen railroad station, following a yellow "Wanderweg" sign to Zweilütschinen and Wilderswill. A narrow path takes *Easy Walkers* past a small barn, near the car road. The rapidly flowing Lütschine is on the right. In about 10 minutes, cross a bridge over the river, and turn left to walk on a path with the river now on the left. This is a particularly wide and comfortable path, with an easy downhill gradient.

After 10 to 15 minutes, you'll see a small cluster of buildings on the left side of the river. While there is a small bridge crossing the river, do not take it today—it leads to the Isenfluh chairlift. (See Walk #5.) Walk straight ahead to "Zweilütschinen - 40 min." and "Wilderswil - 1 hr., 50 min." The path continues to be marked with the familiar yellow "Wanderweg" diamond.

After about an hour of pleasant walking, the outskirts of Zweilütschinen and its railroad station appear. At this point there are options based on the weather. If the weather is very inclement, *Easy Walkers* can take the train back to Lauterbrunnen, or go on to Interlaken. Remember, Zweilütschinen is also the station for the train to Grindelwald.

Proceeding on the planned itinerary, walk through the railroad station, noting the sign marked, "Wilderswil." The wide path follows the railroad tracks for a while, then rises to the right, through the meadows and toward the small town of Gsteigwiler. This is a picturesque village and a bit off the beaten path. There is no train station here and the town is accessible only by car or PTT bus. Walk on the road through the center of town, continuing in the direction of the Wilderswil railroad station. At the outskirts of Gsteigwiler, a sign informs you that Wilderswil is 20 minutes ahead. Continue on this yellow diamond "Wanderweg" path, through forest and meadow. The trail eventually crosses over the Schynige Platte railway line. (See Excursion #7.) After descending on this forest path, the houses of Wilderswil appear in the valley. Follow the road to the church of Gsteig, originally built in 1133, and cross over a charming wooden bridge, taking the middle of three roads to the Wilderswil railroad station.

There are options in Wilderswil for *Easy Walkers*, again depending on the weather. Continue by train to Interlaken, return by train to Lauterbrunnen, or walk to Interlaken.

Many signs at the Wilderswil railroad station indicate directions to Interlaken. Follow "Interlaken - 45 min.," also the way to the castle ruins, going in the same direction. The road takes you up and away from the station. After walking on the main street of Wilderswil for about 10 minutes, pass to the right of the Alpenblick Hotel, and then turn right to, "Interlaken - 40 min." You'll shortly reach a hotel and what appears to be the end of the street. Take the path to the right, and you are on the way to Interlaken and the old castle. If you haven't already raided your backpack, the castle grounds are a wonderful place to have lunch, rest and enjoy the view.

Return to the path, eventually leading into an automobile road. Turn left on this road, walking against traffic, as you are now in the outskirts of Interlaken. You'll pass through the buildings of the Rugenbrau brewery, and you might check to see if it is open for a visit. After passing the Wald Hotel note another sign posted "Interlaken West - 20 min." This route continues to use a combination of road and forest path until you reach the Heimweifluh funicular to the model railway. (See Excursion #2.) Continue straight ahead for 10 minutes—the Interlaken West railroad station and the main shopping area of Interlaken come into view. Take some time to browse through the shops and hotels of Interlaken.

To return to Lauterbrunnen, walk 20 minutes to the Interlaken Ost station, on the main shopping street. Or, return to the Interlaken West station, take the train one stop to Interlaken Ost, and change for the train to Lauterbrunnen.

Walk #8: Excursion to Thun & Walk to the Lake Towns

 Walking Time - 1-3 hours

The city of Thun is an ideal location, not only when the weather is fair, but also when it's cloudy or drizzling or not conducive to higher altitude walking. Thun is the largest and most important town in the Bernese Oberland, situated on the beautiful Thunersee, and easily reached by train from Lauterbrunnen. It has a delightful "old town" section, and a castle that currently serves as a museum. While there are high altitude walks around Thun, we're bringing you there in less than ideal weather because the lakeside walks around Thun can help to brighten a dreary day.

Although Thun is known as a medieval city, the earliest settlement can be traced as far back as 2,500 B.C. The territory was eventually ceded to the Romans, and the name "Thun" was derived from the Latin "Dunum," meaning "Fortified Hill." Thun's imposing castle, set high above and overlooking the city, dominates the town and the lake.

Directions: Buy a round trip Lauterbrunnen to Thun ticket, and take the train from Lauterbrunnen to Interlaken Ost, changing for the train to Thun. The local Tourist Information

Office, designated by a letter "i", is at the end of the railroad station. Maps of the city are available.

As you leave the railroad station and enter the main shopping district, follow the signs with a symbol of a castle. After a 15-minute walk, enter the castle area through ancient fortress walls that date back to the 12th century. The castle is now the property of Bern, and is the seat of various district officials. The main center of attraction is the Knight's Hall, a large room, panelled in tapestries, with a fine collection of weapons used in the 15th century. Other items of interest in the castle include collections of furniture, toys, ceramics, archeological finds, military memorabilia and agricultural implements. Admission is 4 SF.

After exploring and enjoying Thun's medieval castle, walk down and around the hill, back toward the railroad station and the canal you crossed earlier. Note a group of yellow signs with

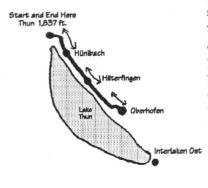

directions for walks along scenic Lake Thun. Turn left in the direction of "Oberhofen" and walk on the wide paved path along the canal, leaving the center of Thun. Take special notice of the beautiful estates fronting on the canal and lake, with well-tended and colorful gardens. Thun is at your back, with the turreted castle dominating the horizon. After walking 40 minutes, you'll see the small pier and ticket office for the regularly scheduled steamer stop at Hunibach. A short walk to the left brings *Easy Walkers* to the main street, with a choice of restaurants. After lunch there are two options, again depending on the weather. Follow the same lake path back to Thun and take the train to Interlaken Ost and Lauterbrunnen. Or, on leaving Hunibach, walk in the direction of Hilterfingen, where there is another castle—Castle Hunegg, built a century ago—and more elaborate than Thun castle. It is beautifully situated in a park-like setting, with the small village and its mountains as a backdrop. From Hilterfingen, follow the directional signs to Oberhofen and a medieval castle which houses weapons, toys and musical instruments from Bern's Historical Museum. On the castle grounds is an alpine garden with fine views over Lake Thun.

Hunibach, Hilterfingen and Oberhofen are all regularly scheduled steamer stops for the return to Thun, where you can change for the train to Interlaken Ost—or ahead to Interlaken West where you can change for the train to Interlaken Ost. If the weather is not conducive to a steamer trip, a PTT bus services all the towns and can be taken back to Thun and the railroad station.

Easy Walkers will find Thun a picturesque city, retaining much of its medieval character and charm—and an excellent center for a number of fascinating walks around the lake.

Sample Timetable to Thun:

Lauterbrunnen	9:08 am dep.
Interlaken Ost	9:30 am arr.
Interlaken Ost	9:38 am dep.
Thun	10:10 am arr.

Walk #9: Kleine Scheidegg to Alpiglen to Brandegg to Grindelwald

     Walking Time - 3 1/2 hours

This trip is best taken on a clear day, as the views are mesmerizing. Thousands of walkers visit Kleine Scheidegg, the crossroads at the top of the world, to continue up to the magical ice kingdom of the Jungfrau, or to walk gently up to Männlichen for a journey to either Grindelwald or Wengen.

Any path you choose is in the shadow of the 13,642 ft. Jungfrau, and the foreboding, north face of the 13,025 ft. Eiger. You will see the Jungfrau Railway, an engineering miracle of the century, as it climbs from Kleine Scheidegg at 6,760 ft., through the Mönch, to the Jungfraujoch at 11,333 ft. The path down from Kleine Scheidegg to Grindelwald is mostly in the open, eventually bringing you through meadows for a descent into Grindelwald.

Directions: Pack your picnic lunch and purchase a train ticket from Lauterbrunnen to Kleine Scheidegg, with a return from Grindelwald to Lauterbrunnen via Zweilütschinen. After a 20-minute ride to Wengen, the train continues to Kleine Scheidegg where the walk begins.

Start: Outside this busy station, is a group of yellow signs, one of which directs you to "Alpiglen - 1 hr." and "Grindelwald - 2 1/2 hrs." As you walk down this path, additional signs confirm your direction. Grindelwald is in the distant valley, with the train from Kleine Scheidegg on the right. The path descends 3,300 ft. over the 3 hours time it will take to walk to Grindelwald. At this point we'll remind *Easy Walkers* to rest frequently, keeping the pressure off your knees, and giving ample time to

Start Here
Kleine Scheidegg
6,762 ft.

Alpiglen
5,199 ft.

End Here
Grindelwald
3,393 ft.

Brandegg
4,370 ft.

Grindelwald Grund
3,094 ft.

take in the breathtaking scenery, as you head through the valley, on a well-signed, easy to follow path.

After an hour, cross the railroad tracks, and look to the rear—the Männlichen cable station is in the far distance on its plateau. Within a few minutes, you will reach the Alpiglen Restaurant, with directions to the Alpiglen Station for a quick train ride to Grindelwald, or to Brandegg and Grindelwald by foot. Continuing the walk, you'll shortly come to a fork in the path and a sign to the right indicating, "Steiler Abstieg nach Grindelwald," a steep descent. We recommend continuing straight ahead, following the signs to "Brandegg Station" and "Grindelwald."

From this point on, the path intertwines with a narrow car road, easily traversed by following the friendly yellow diamond

"Wanderweg" blazes. When not walking on sections of the auto road, you'll be going down fenced, narrow paths. At a major auto road, turn right to "Grindelwald-Dorf - 25 min.," bringing you to the main shopping district and the railroad station.

Trains to Lauterbrunnen leave 20 minutes and 50 minutes past the hour—remember to change in Zweilütschinen for the Lauterbrunnen train.

Walk #10:   Pfingstegg to Stieregg to Pfingstegg to Cafe Milchbach to Hotel Wetterhorn (to Grindelwald)

Walking Time - 4 hours
5 hours with option

There's a double treat in store for *Easy Walkers* today. After taking the cable car from Grindelwald to Pfingstegg, the trail will proceed 984 ft. up to Stieregg at 5,577 ft., for a close look at the Unter Grindelwald Glacier. The ascent can be demanding, but the mountain path is well-defined and can be traversed easily, at your own pace. The reward is the overview of the first of two glaciers that *Easy Walkers* will visit on this hike.

After returning to Pfingstegg, the path descends 1,500 ft. to the Cafe Milchbach, and the Ober Grindelwald Glacier, the second glacier visited, with the possibility of walking into the glacier's ice caves. The hike ends with a walk to the Hotel Wetterhorn, and a short bus ride back to the Grindelwald station.

Directions: After packing your picnic lunch, purchase a round-trip ticket to Grindelwald via Zweilütschinen. Take the train to Grindelwald and walk up the main shopping street, stopping at the "i" in the Sports Zentrum Building on the right to pick up a walking map of Grindelwald and any other information you would like to have about this area.

Continuing on the main street, a sign directs you to the right, marked "Pfingstegg Bahn." Purchase a one-way ticket to the 4,564 ft. Pfingstegg station, with a restaurant and facilities. Follow the sign, "Stieregg - 1 hr." to the right, and you are on your way up this "bergweg," overlooking all of Grindelwald, and heading to Stieregg and the glacier. This path is blazed white-red-white, with no chance for confusion, and we remind *Easy Walkers* to proceed at your own comfortable pace. Proceeding up the trail, the leading edge of the glacier becomes visible, and Männlichen can be seen on top of the mountains to the right. Within 1 1/2 hours you'll reach the plateau over-looking the glacier, and descend gently to the restaurant at Stieregg, completing the first part of today's double glacier visit.

Return by retracing your steps to Pfingstegg, about an hour of downhill walking, and continue by following the sign to "Milchbach" and "Hotel Wetterhorn." The rest of today's walk is mostly downhill, except for a short rise before reaching the

Oberer Gletscher at Cafe Milchbach. This path to Milchbach and Grindelwald continues to be well signed, and is highlighted by rock formations revealing deposits representing a time gap of 80 million years—a "geologist's paradise."

Follow directions to the Cafe Milchbach, with a sun-terrace overlooking the leading edge of the glacier. From there, walk down to the "Hotel Wetterhorn - 20 min.," by way of the Blue Grotto Ice Caves. A visit to these caves costs 4 SF and allows you to walk through man-made tunnels into the glacier itself, highlighting the brilliant, azure blue color.

Continue on the same path to the Hotel Wetterhorn, and within 15 minutes, cross a wide gravel auto road leading into the parking lot across from the hotel. Buy a bus ticket for the short ride back to the Grindelwald station, or, if you still feel fit, walk through the parking lot to your left, and follow a sign directing you through meadow and forest for a pleasant, 1-hour walk back to Grindelwald.

KANDERSTEG

Kandersteg has everyone and everything going for it—a central location with a plethora of quality walks, full train and bus service, the beautiful Gastern Valley (Gasterntal), and proximity to the Lötschberg Tunnel for quick access to southern Switzerland with the unique Lötschental's impressive glaciers and centuries old villages. If that's not enough, the lakeside towns of Thun, Interlaken and Spiez are only a short train ride away, and Zermatt—home of the Matterhorn and Gornergrat—is an easy day excursion.

Kandersteg, at 3,793 ft., sits in a narrow, fertile valley, sandwiched between high mountain peaks, and boasts a particularly active Tourist "i" Office. There is good availability of hotels, but early reservations are usually neccessary, as Kandersteg is well-used by hikers and hiking groups.

Excursions from Kandersteg include a variety of low, medium and high-level walks on a large network of well-maintained trails. Visit the remarkable Blausee, a small, crystal-clear lake in a wondrous, natural setting; walk on the heights around Kandersteg, with views of the snow-covered, Blümlisalp mountain range; hike along the raging Kander torrent through the Kander Gorge; and marvel at the unspoiled beauty of the Gasterntal. The mountains above Kandersteg lead from the Gemmi Pass down to the charming spa village of Leukerbad; or to the Oeschinensee, a glacial lake set under high cliff walls, easily accessible by chairlift.

Kandersteg is a hiker's paradise. Walkers return year after year to this lovely, centrally located Bernese Oberland village. Hotels are comfortable, walks are numerous, and the scenery is breathtaking—a perfect setting for *Walking Easy in the Swiss Alps.*

Transportation

Zurich Airport to Kandersteg - After clearing Swiss Customs, follow the sign to the "Bahnhof," marked with a symbol of a train. Stop at any ticket window to validate your Swiss Pass or Swiss Card. Take one of the frequent trains to Zurich Central and change for the train to Bern, checking the large, overhead information panels for the time and track number. In Bern, change for the train to Kandersteg. For the best views of Lake Thun on this portion of the trip, sit on the left side of the car, facing front.

If you are traveling to Kandersteg from a point in Switzerland or Europe other than Zurich, please check local connections. A trip from points south, such as Zermatt or Saas-Fee, involves a change of train in Brig.

Sample Timetable:

Zurich Airport to Zurich Central	Take any train
Zurich Central to Bern	11:03 am dep.
Bern	12:14 pm arr.
Bern to Kandersteg	12:22 pm dep.
Kandersteg	13:22 pm arr. (1:22 PM)

Activities in Kandersteg

This section lists activities available in Kandersteg on days when additions or alternatives to walking are desired. Please check with the Kandersteg Tourist Bureau, Tel:75 12 34, for current details on all activities. It is located on the main street, diagonally across from the Chalet-Hotel Adler. All Kandersteg guests receive a Visitors Card when registering at their hotel— to be used for discounts on many activities and cable lifts.

- Swimming - heated pool with whirlpool, call 75 14 62, 4 SF. Lake swimming at Oeschinensee.
- Ice Skating - at rink near train station.
- Fishing - trout fishing at Oeschinensee. Check with the Tourist Bureau for permit information.

- Tennis - sand courts at Hotels Royal Bellevue and Schweizer-hof - 15 SF/hour. Artificial courts at the Victoria & Ritter - 14 SF/hour.
- Bowling - at the Hotels Blümlisalp and Zur Post.
- Vita Parcours (keep Fit Course) - begins in the forest behind the Catholic Church.
- Miniature Golf
- Boating - pedalos and row boats at the Oeschinensee.
- Paragliding - Allmenalp Paragliding School, Call 75 19 17 for information.
- Horseback Riding - Hotel Royal Bellevue, Call 75 12 12, 32 SF/hour.
- Wildlife Spotting - with guide every Wednesday. Contact Tourist Office.
- Organ Concerts - every Monday evening at 8:45 pm, at the Protestant Church.
- Botanical Tours - with guide every Wednesday. Contact Tourist Office.
- Folklore Evenings - once a month in the school playground or Congress Hall. Notices posted around town.
- Drinks and Music - 5 to 6 pm, 2nd Monday of each summer month, in front of the Tourist Office.

Excursions in and Around Kandersteg

This section introduces day-excursions for *Easy Walkers* to enjoy when the weather is not suitable for high-altitude walking, or when an alternative to walking is desired. Be sure to check local timetables for best connections if using public transportation.

1. Oeschinensee Chairlift (Kandersteg) - Take the 9-minute chairlift ride to the upper station and walk 20 minutes to Lake Oeschinen on a wide, forest path. This clear mountain lake is at the foot of the Blümlisalps. Restaurant and sun-terrace are available, rent a pedal boat, or enjoy a picnic lunch.

Directions to Oeschinensee: Walk north on the main street. Past the Tourist Office are signs directing you to the right to the chairlift.

2. Sunnbüel Cable Car (Kandersteg) - This cable car rises in 7 minutes from Eggeschwand—a short walk or bus ride from Kandersteg—to the natural "sunbowl" or Sunnbüel at the top station. A restaurant with a sun-terrace overlooking this beautiful, high valley is a few minutes walk.

Directions to Sunnbüel: Walk south on the main street, past the Hotel Schweizerhof, and follow the "Stock-Gemmi" signs for the 30-minute walk to Eggeschwand. Or, take the city bus at any stop—schedules are posted.

3. Allmenalp - An 8-person gondola lifts visitors to 5,683 ft. in 5 minutes. Allmenalp offers views into the Kander Valley, up to Oeschinensee and its towering cliffs. A small cheese dairy operates in back of the restaurant in the morning, and paragliders take off from the nearby meadow. Fare is 11 SF round-trip.

Directions: Pick up the signs to the "Allmenalp Luftseil-bahn" in town or by the railroad station, and walk 20 minutes to the lift station.

4. Blausee - The clear blue color of Blausee is exceptionally beautiful, and this small lake sits amid a network of paths that wind around and through the magnificent surrounding forests. A visit to the Trout Breeding Station and St. Bernard kennels is particularly interesting, as is a boat ride around this glacial lake. (See Walk #2.)

Directions to Blausee: Take the bus from Kandersteg to Blausee. The bus schedule and bus stop are posted in front of the railroad station.

5. Spiez - This charming town on the shore of Lake Thun, is easily accessible from Kandersteg. Its medieval castle, built in the 12th and 13th centuries, overlooks the lake and vineyards. Various rooms have been turned into a museum, with Gothic, Renaissance and Baroque furniture predominating. Open Tuesday through Sunday, admission is 3 SF.

Paths take *Easy Walkers* along Lake Thun in both directions. The path to "Faulensee," a small sailing resort, is found across from the castle, and an interesting walk to "Gwatt" begins near the castle. (See Walk #9.)

Directions to Spiez: Trains to Spiez run 37 minutes past the hour from Kandersteg station, and return from Spiez to Kandersteg at 54 minutes past every hour, for the 1/2 hour-trip.

6. Thun - The medieval city of Thun lies at the northern end of Lake Thun, with its cobblestone streets and famous castle. Thun is also the center for a number of walks around the lake after exploring the "old town." (See Walk #8 in Lauterbrunnen section.) Check with the Tourist Bureau in the Thun railroad station for a city sightseeing map.

Directions to Thun: The train to Thun, via Spiez, leaves Kandersteg 37 minutes past every hour for the 40-minute trip. From Thun, the train returns to Kandersteg 43 minutes past the hour.

7. Bern - The capital of Switzerland is a delightful city of medieval arches, fountains, towers, an ancient clock tower and, of course, the famous bear pits the city is named after. You will enjoy shopping and sightseeing in this typically Swiss city with a small town feeling. The Bern Tourist Office is located in the railroad station (follow the "i" signs), and will supply you with maps and sightseeing suggestions.

Directions to Bern: Take the direct train to Bern, leaving Kandersteg 37 minutes past the hour, for a 1-hour ride, and return from Bern to Kandersteg at 22 minutes past every hour.

8. Interlaken - Interlaken, named for its location between Lake Thun and Lake Brienz, is a busy tourist center, surrounded by a superb mountain panorama. The Höheweg, a wide street bustling with stores, restaurants and hotels, links the east (ost) section of Interlaken with the busy west area. Interlaken's casino (Kursaal), is on the Höheweg, past the splendid Hotel Victoria-Jungfrau, and should be visited to admire its colorful gardens and large, floral clock. The lake steamer piers are outside both the Interlaken Ost station for a ride on Lake Brienz, or the Interlaken West station for the trip on Lake Thun.

Heimwehfluh, a 5-minute walk from the Interlaken West train station, features an elaborate scale-model railway, and is reached by funicular railroad. Harder Kulm, reached by another funicular, is a 5-minute walk from the Interlaken Ost station. At the summit are several well-marked trails, a restaurant, facilities and large sun-terrace.

Directions to Interlaken Ost or Interlaken West: Take the train from Kandersteg to Spiez, and change for the train to Interlaken. To return to Kandersteg, take any train leaving Interlaken Ost or Interlaken West, and change in Spiez for the return to Kandersteg.

9. Leukerbad - This spa, or "bad," is set at 4,600 ft. in a huge punchbowl surrounded by high mountains. Leukerbad's warm water springs are reputed to be the hottest in Switzerland, with many therapeutic properties attributed to them. In the 19th century, a visit to this spa was considered a must for travelers, and Mark Twain depicted these people in his book, *Tramp Abroad*. From Leukerbad, visitors can take a cable car to the Gemmi Pass, with wondrous views of the region. (See Walk #6.)

Directions to Leukerbad: From Kandersteg, take a train to Brig, changing in Brig for the train to Leuk, where you catch the bus to Leukerbad. All connections are within 10 minutes, and the 8:24 am train to Brig brings you to Leukerbad at 10:15 am. To return to Kandersteg, take the bus from Leukerbad to Leuk, catching the train to Brig and changing for the train to Kandersteg. If you take the 3:40 pm bus from Leukerbad, *Easy Walkers* will be in Kandersteg at 5:37 pm.

10. Stresa, Italy - Stresa is a beautiful Italian village, situated on Lake Maggiore, facing the incredible Borromean Islands. The most famous of the islands is Isola Bella (Beautiful Island), and your train ticket includes a tour through its extraordinary gardens and palace.

Directions to Stresa, Italy: The "Stresa Express" runs every summer Tuesday. It leaves Kandersteg station at 8:30 am, arrives in Stresa at 10:30 am. The ferry leaves for Isola Bella 11:00 am and arrives 11:10 am. The ticket price (check at the train station) includes the train, boat and tour of the castle with a multilingual guide. The train leaves Stresa at 4:25 pm and returns to Kandersteg at 7:10 pm. Make reservations in ad-

vance at the train station. **Remember to take yo**
passport!

11. Zermatt - Zermatt is a tourist and hiking mecca encompassing some of the world's most superb scenery, including the mighty Matterhorn. You can spend the day walking in the busy, car-free streets of Zermatt, with their mix of souvenir shops and cosmopolitan boutiques, or choose any of the following sightseeing options:

   A. Gornergrat Cog Railway - entrance across the street from the Zermatt train station. Takes *Easy Walkers* to Gornergrat at 10,272 ft., 1 1/2 hrs. round-trip travel time; and Stockhorn at 11,588 ft., a 45-minute round trip cable car ride from Gornergrat.

   B. Klein Matterhorn Cable Car - a 20-minute walk from the Zermatt train station, following the signs through town. Allow 2 hours roundtrip travel time on the four different and connecting cable cars to reach 12,684 ft.; or change at the Furgg station for the 3-minute trip to Schwarzsee, at the foot of the Matterhorn.

   C. Sunnegga Underground Railway - after arriving at the Zermatt train station, walk straight ahead, following the signs to the Sunnegga Express station. This underground railway takes 20 minutes to reach the high, alpine plateau of Sunnegga at 7,500 ft. From Sunnegga, a cable car continues up to Blauherd at 8,620 ft., and the Unterrothorn at 10,180 ft.

   All these trains and cable cars offer exceptional views of the Matterhorn and other area peaks. (See Excursion #6 in Zermatt Section.)

   Directions to Zermatt: The 1 3/4 hour trip from Kandersteg to Zermatt includes a change of train in Brig. The 8:24 am train arrives in Zermatt at 10:47 am. To return to Kandersteg, trains leave Zermatt for Brig at 10 minutes past every hour, and the 3:10 pm train brings *Easy Walkers* back to Kandersteg at 6:12 pm, after a change in Brig.

Walks

Walk #1: Selden to Heimritz to Selden to Waldhaus to Kandersteg (through the Gastern Valley)

Walking Time - 3 to 4 hours

There's a treat in store for you today. The Gasterntal has been here for centuries, well before Walt Disney created his "Magic Kingdom," but it surely must mean that Mr. Disney visited this dream valley for creative inspiration.

The "magic kingdom" you will visit today is called the Gasterntal or Gastern Valley, ending at the leading edge of a great glacier, the source of the Kander River, which flows all the way to Lake Thun.

Travel to Selden from Kandersteg is by mini-bus, along a marvelously engineered mountain road, so narrow that it requires traffic control by a series of stop lights at the bottom and the top.

Note to *Easy Walkers*: Bus reservations should be made one day in advance, by calling 75 16 26.

After arriving at Selden, 5,036 ft., walkers will continue up the valley to Heimritz, 5,364 ft., with its tiny *gasthaus* and views of the leading edge of the glacier. You'll return by walking to Kandersteg on well-signed paths, through shaded forests, and grassy meadows, never far from the rushing Kander River, and finally past the Kander Waterfall and spectacular Kander Gorge.

The end of the walk passes the Eggeschwand-Sunnbüel Lift, for the return to Kandersteg.

Directions: The day before this trip is planned, make reservations with the mini-bus company, riding **to** Selden, and walking back to Kandersteg. Restaurants and facilities are available at Selden and Waldhaus, with opportunities for a picnic lunch along the trail. We recommend taking the 9:30 am mini-bus, leaving enough time to enjoy the Gasterntal—as the next bus departs at 10:30 am. Across from the Kandersteg railroad station, a white sign indicates the Selden bus stop, the driver checking for reservations before allowing general entry. A one-way ticket costs 9 SF for the 20-minute ride. Exit the bus in front of the Hotel Steinbock, after a sensational ride on a narrow mountain road through small tunnels, and under ridges of the mountain.

Start: Follow the sign ahead to "Heimritz-20 minutes," on a narrow, paved path towards the distant mountains. The path ascends from 5,043 ft. to 5,364 ft., and is gradual and well-defined. The view on the right is of the Kander River, with high mountains on either side, forming a fertile, long, narrow valley.

Continue straight ahead to Heimritz on the main path, and within 25 minutes you'll reach Gasthaus Gletscher Heimritz. Walk past the gasthaus, and around the bend for several hundred yards, for a magnificent view of the leading edge of the Alpetligletscher. If you wish, continue along the trail toward Kanderfirn, remembering to leave enough time for the scheduled return walk to Kandersteg.

When ready, retrace your steps to Selden for the 2 1/2 hour walk to Kandersteg. The walk begins on the car road, but after 15 minutes signs point left towards "Eggeschwand," "Waldhaus" and "Kandersteg," on a Wanderweg, now blazed with the familiar yellow diamond. The path descends, interrupted by large stretches of even terrain. Crossing the river on a small bridge as directed, exit the forest into an open meadow, with a large sea of larch trees on the right. The Balmhorn is left, with high, jagged, foreboding peaks, reflecting the sun and casting dancing images across the valley floor. Cross the river several times, entering a forest, as the path narrows and descends more rapidly, but always comfortably. The Kander Falls are on the left as you cross the valley floor. Take a minute to turn around and view the scene—the glacier straight ahead, the waterfall to the right, with high, rock walls on either side of the valley. Continue walking through the valley, passing a carved statue of a Swiss climber, pointing to the Balmhornhütte, high up on the mountain, and marked 2 1/2 hours. Follow the signs to "Waldhaus" and "Kandersteg," passing by an electric power station, and within 1 3/4 hours from the start of the walk from Selden, you'll reach the Hotel Waldhaus at 4,456 ft. A stop here allows you to sit on the sun-terrace having a drink, overlooking the entire Gastern Valley.

Continue on the trail, behind the hotel as directed, toward Kandersteg. Reenter the forest, blazed with the friendly yellow wanderweg diamond—through tall pine and fir trees, with a branch of the river on your left. Within 10 minutes you'll enter what appears to be a parking lot, but is actually a reserved space for military vehicles, and if you look up to your left, carved into the face of the mountain, might be openings for Swiss gun emplacements, protecting the narrow valley entrance from intruders.

Walk with the now raging Kander River on your right, and after 15 minutes of descending a rocky path, recross the river. Make sure you've closed the gate behind you, as you enter the Kander Gorge. The roaring river crescendos as it rushes downward through the narrow gorge. You'll walk on the auto road for a short period of time, but as the road turns left to enter a tunnel, a sign takes you to Eggeschwand and Kandersteg on a descending mountain path. This is an exciting part of the walk, traversing the gorge, feeling the power and the spray of the raging torrent. The well-defined path is rocky, so watch your step as you descend, and within a few minutes, the lush, tranquil, green valley beyond Eggeschwand appears.

Cross the bridge to the right, and turn to the left, as the path becomes a car road and enters the parking lot of the Sunnbüel cable car lift.

Easy Walkers have the option of returning to Kandersteg by bus, or continuing on a delightful walk through town.

Walk #2:   Kandersteg to Blausee to Kandergrund (excursion to Blausee—Blue Lake)

   Walking Time - 2 1/2 hours

The walk to Blausee from Kandersteg is a northerly trek along the Kander River, leaving Kandersteg at 3,730 ft., to the beautiful Blausee at 2,910 ft. The path is well-defined, and traverses through shaded forest and open meadow to one of Switzerland's most beautiful natural wonders. Some 15,000 years ago an avalanche shook the Kander Valley and enormous chunks of ice thundered down the mountain. These ice blocks left clefts and filled the resulting hollows with water as they melted, forming the Blausee, or Blue Lake. The Blausee, famous for its trout, is a small lake, about 2 1/2 acres, with a maximum depth of 60 ft. The clear blue color of the lake is due to the exceptional purity of the water, the color of the lake's bottom, and the reflections of its surroundings.

Blausee sits in the middle of a park, boasting a network of walking paths, including the quickly flowing Kander River. A trout breeding station can be visited, with an exceptional family of Saint Bernard dogs. Take the boat ride around the lake, included in your admission ticket price.

Start: After picking up a picnic lunch, walk to the railroad station, where one of a series of signs will direct you to the right (facing the station) through a parking lot, "Blausee-1 hour 15 minutes." As you head north in the direction of Blausee and Frutigen, the Kander River is on the right. One explanation for the cleanliness of this path, and others in Switzerland, is a little story worth telling. As we proceeded on this lovely, shaded, well-kept path, we noticed a small sign on the left side of the path ahead of us reading, "WC." We thought, "How thoughtful for the local authorities to provide facilities along the way." But as we approached the sign we realized it was not for humans but for our four-legged friend, the dog! The sign announced,

"This WC is for your pet." And there, at the side of the trail was a large scoop, a roll of plastic bags, and a covered pail, with signs beseeching passers-by to use these facilities for man's best friend. Knowing the needs of Swiss pets were taken care of, we went on towards Blausee, feeling very good about the city fathers.

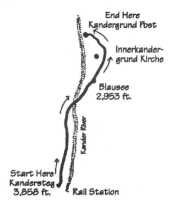

In about 10 minutes the path splits, but stay on the right along the river. Continue on this yellow-blazed Wanderweg, under the railroad tracks, past the power station, still walking along the river, following the sign to "Blausee-1 hour." After 40 minutes of walking you'll reach the tiny town of Unter Buhl. If for any reason there is a problem and you wish to return to Kandersteg, make a right turn at the sign, arriving at a bus stop in 5 minutes for scheduled bus service back to Kandersteg.

Continue straight ahead on this main path. Signs indicate "Blausee-35 minutes," "Kandergrund-50 minutes," and "Frutigen-2 hrs. 15 minutes." Follow the trail to Blausee, down the hill to your right, leaving the path that continues on to Frutigen. Crossing over the river, passing some private homes, *Easy Walkers* will reach the main auto road, with signs pointing across the highway and left. Within 10 minutes, notice the sign announcing "Blausee-the Blue Lake," back across the road to the left.

Walk through the parking lot to reach the entrance, and pay a fee of 4 SF, entitling you to visit the trout nursery. Spend at least 1 1/2 hours visiting this lovely park, taking a boat ride, walking through the trout hatchery, enjoying your picnic lunch at the tables provided and wandering on some of the forest paths. If the urge to have fresh trout overcomes you, a trout lunch at the restaurant costs about 24 SF. Facilities are provided at the side of the restaurant.

Leave Blausee by the rock path, ending just past the entrance booth, for the walk back to the road. Make a left turn on the sidewalk at the auto road, and continue down the hill towards Kandergrund. A few minutes after passing the Zoo Tierpark, a sign across the road points to "Wanderweg-Kandergrund." Take that path, walking through the meadow, in the direction of "Inner Kandergrund Kirche." As you pass the church and arrive at intersecting paths, walk up the hill to the right, in the direction of "Frutigen," "Spitzruteli" and "Kandergrund." The trail goes up into the forest, offering spectacular views of the valley below—rolling green meadows, dotted with small villages—surrounded by the cacophony of Swiss cow bells. Following a sign, "Kandergrund Station-20 minutes," turn sharply left, on a narrow, meadow path.

This path continues to be blazed by the friendly yellow wanderweg diamond, and enters the forest for a descending mountain trail to Kandergrund. This well-beaten path takes you through a turnstile and within a short time meets a paved auto road. Walk left, and through a tunnel under the railroad tracks, where the road enters the hardly-used Kandergrund railroad station. A sign points down a paved, sharply zigzagging path, to the Kandergrund PTT bus stop. Cross the road by an old barn and wait for the bus to Kandersteg, running 20 minutes past the hour.

Walk #3: Kandersteg to Höhwald to Kandersteg (along the Höh, the heights around Kandersteg) (excursion to Allmenalp)

 Walking Time - 2 1/2 hours

    This walk offers some of the most dramatic scenery around the little town of Kandersteg. *Easy Walkers* will look down on Kandersteg, nestled along the Kander River, with views of the surrounding mountains from many different perspectives. A gondola rises to Allmenalp, a plateau under the Bundespitz with a cheese-making dairy and restaurant—a favorite jumping off place for paragliders.

    After returning by gondola to the valley floor, the walk continues on the "Höhweg" along the Kandersteg heights, walking on different types of terrain, from well-engineered, wide paths, to narrow "mountain goat" trails; through sun-filled grassy meadows, and rocky, shaded, forest bergwegs.

    Start: Facing the Kandersteg station, turn left through the tunnel under the tracks, and left again, so that you are walking south with the tracks on your left. This signed path goes directly to the Allmenalp *luftseilbahn*. The private homes on either side of the path seem to compete, with an abundance of colorful garden and window box flowers. After 20 minutes of walking with the waterfall on your right, the path swerves directly towards the waterfall and the lift base station.

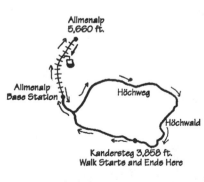

If the weather is clear, you may see dozens of paragliders coming off the top of the Allmenalp as you walk by their landing field.

The lift station is at 3,891 ft., and the small, 8-passenger gondola rises to 5,683 ft. in 5 minutes This lift is privately owned, not honoring Swiss discount transportation passes. Buy a round trip ticket for 11 SF, and enter the gondola, closing the door behind you. At the top station, open the door after the car has stopped, and exit the small, unattended station. To return, raise the receiver at the station, turn the crank a few times, press a button, and inform the base station you are ready to return. Step into the car, closing the door behind you, allowing no more than 8 persons in the small cabin. A bell will ring, and within a minute the gondola starts to descend.

On Allmenalp, visit the little cheesemaking dairy next to the restaurant, and walk to the lookout point for a spectacular view of the Kander Valley, all the way to the Oechinensee, surrounded by high cliffs. There are several walks, including one that goes over the mountain for a six-hour trek to Adelboden, and a circuitous trail that descends down to the valley floor. But we suggest returning by gondola to continue walking along the heights bordering Kandersteg.

Leave the base station and retrace your steps on the paved road, making a first left on another road marked "privat strasse," with a sign reading "Dhammapala." Peer around the other side of the sign to read it—as it's only printed on one side. Make a left on this road as it proceeds through the meadow, passing the Waldrand ski lift on the right, walking in the direction of the waterfall. The road empties into a small parking lot with a large, flower-bedecked house inscribed, "Buddist Kloster, Dhammapala." This charming brown weathered chalet is run by Buddhist monks, and provides spiritual meditation for visitors.

A small grassy path enters the forest on the left side of the cloister, and after 10 minutes, the trail breaks out of the woods, passing a small wooden barn on the right, continuing left to "Höh Panoramaweg." There is an option at this crossing to cut the walk short by turning right, down to Bütschels and eventually, Kandersteg.

Within a few minutes the mountain ranges that give this valley its special flavor, come into view. The jagged peak of the

Doldenhorn overlooks the valley up on the right. The trail continues north through this alp, with many waterfalls and pine forests, under the snow-covered peaks. As you ascend gradually on this Panoramaweg, look back at the magnificent view of the entrance into the Gastern Valley.

A sign points to a narow mountain trail to the left, marked "Höh and Golitschenalp." After unhooking a springed wire fence latch and closing it behind you, walk around a farm and up a small hill—this trail leading to a high point for all-encompassing views to the south and west. The yellow diamond Wanderweg meanders on a beaten, grassy path through the meadow, entering several wooden gates as you cross gently from one pasture to another.

Take the path down to the right marked "Kandersteg Waldweg-30 minutes," cross the wagon road, and pass to the right of a small cabin, entering into a forest area. Within a minute the yellow, diamond-blazed trail splits. Take the left trail for a descent to the road below. Turn left on the road in the direction of "Bühl" and "Kandersteg." The road winds around the mountain, and at a major intersection marked "Kandersteg" to the right and "Blausee" to the left, turn **left**, as if to Blausee, and then make an immediate right. Walk through the power station and tunnel, under the highway, continuing on the path to Kandersteg station, with the river on your left.

Walk #4:   Kandersteg to Eggeschwand, Sunnbüel to Spittelmatte to Schwarenbach to Sunnbüel (see Walk #5 - another option)

 Walking Time - 3 1/2 hours

This walk should be made on a clear day, as the alps and mountain ranges on either side of this path are truly spectacular. Your first part of the trip is the walk from Kandersteg to Eggeschwand, where you'll board the cable car for the 7-minute ride up to the 6,345 ft. Sunnbüel station. The walk is on a well-defined, wide path for the entire trip, with many walkers moving in all directions. You'll walk through the Spittelmatte meadows for the steady climb to Schwarenbach, at 6,762 ft., with a hotel, restaurant and facilities.

Walkers can continue past Schwarenbach, to the Daubensee at 7,238 ft., eventually walking over the Gemmi Pass at 7,710 ft. Today, however, after refreshments and a picnic lunch, you'll return on the same path, descending to Kandersteg by cable car.

Start: Pack your picnic lunch and the ever present bottle of water, departing central Kandersteg by way of the sidewalk on the main street, heading south. A brown and white sign marked "Stock Gemmi" will direct you past the Hotel

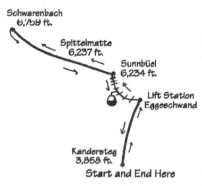

Schweizerhof. Follow the sidewalk to Eggeschwand, arriving at the base station for the Sunnbüel Luftseilbahn within 30 minutes. Buy a round trip ticket, and a cable car will rise to Sunnbüel in 7 minutes. Walk ahead, following a sign to "Spittelmatte - 15 minutes," passing under a ski lift, and proceeding down and through the meadow, as if walking through the center of a large punchbowl. After 15 minutes of walking in the flat meadow, a working dairy farm on your right is worth a visit. There are picnic tables in front of the barn, and a bench up on a small hill to the left, where *Easy Walkers* can picnic before proceeding back on the main path towards Schwarenbach.

The path ascends, with directions "Hotel Schwarenbach-30 minutes" painted on a rock. Don't believe it! Fifty minutes is more realistic, as this wide, comfortable path ascends more steeply to reach Schwarenbach at 6,759 ft. While the views are not spectacular from this point, the restaurant is a good place to rest, have some refreshment, and prepare for the return trip via the same path, to the Sunnbüel cable car, down to Eggeschwand, and the walk back to central Kandersteg.

Please check Walk #5 for another version of this walk—a rewarding full day's excursion and walk over the Gemmi Pass, from Leukerbad. You wouldn't want to do both walks—just one or the other.

Walk #5: Gemmi Pass to Daubensee to Schwarenbach to Sunnbüel (excursion to Leukerbad)

Walking Time - 3 1/2 hours

An interesting full day's excursion is planned, as you leave Kandersteg by early train for Brig, changing for a train westbound to Leuk, the bus to Leukerbad and then taking the Leukerbad-Gemmi lift, rising from 4,630 ft. to the pass at 7,710 ft. This excursion offers downhill walking most of the way, with the sun at your back for an early afternoon walk. The walk begins at the lift station, past the Daubensee at 7,240 ft., continuing a downhill trek on a well-defined path to Schwarenbach at 6,762 ft. You will continue through the Spittelmatte meadow to the Sunnbüel lift station at 6,345 ft., riding the cable car down to Eggeschwand for the 30-minute walk back to Kandersteg where you began the trip earlier this morning.

For those who don't wish to travel by train and bus to Leukerbad, please see an abridged version in Walk #4.

Directions: Buy a ticket from Kandersteg to the Gemmi Lift, with return on the Sunnbüel cable car to Kandersteg. We suggest taking the 8:24 am train from Kandersteg to Brig, changing for the train to Leuk. Outside the Leuk station, take the bus to Leukerbad, and spend time visiting this very lovely, high altitude spa village. (See Excursion #9.) When ready to leave, take the Gemmi lift for the start of the walk.

Start: From the Pass at 7,710 ft., walk down to the Daubensee, following signs outside the Gemmi Pass lift station. Proceed along the lake to a path marked "Schwarenbach." This part of the walk should take about 1 hour. Schwarenbach is a small hotel, with restaurant and facilities, and after a short rise, the path descends through the Spittelmatte meadows to Sunnbüel. Take the lift down to the base station at Eggeschwand, where *Easy Walkers* have the option of walking 30 minutes to Kandersteg, or waiting for the bus which leaves from the parking lot at the base station.

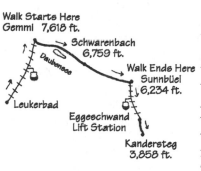

Walk Starts Here
Gemmi 7,618 ft.

Schwarenbach
6,759 ft.

Daubensee

Walk Ends Here
Sunnbüel
6,234 ft.

Leukerbad

Eggeschwand
Lift Station

Kandersteg
3,858 ft.

Walk #6: Schwandfeldspitz to Adelboden (excursion to Adelboden)

   Walking Time - 2 hours

Adelboden is a mountain village in the Bernese Oberland facing southwest, ensuring plenty of sunshine in this ski and walking resort. While only 3,500 people inhabit this friendly mountain village, it burgeons to tens of thousands in the height of the winter and summer seasons.

Today's walk will take you from the top of the Schwandfeldspitz, along the Tschenten Alp, over meadow and mountain path, mostly downhill, with beautiful views in all directions—a good way to become acquainted with walking in the Adelboden area. The trail crosses over the Hörnli, following the Hornliweg, across mountain pastures, and down shaded forest trails.

At Hörnli you will descend on a comfortable wagon path into Adelboden, for the bus ride back to Frutigen, and the return train to Kandersteg.

Directions: After packing a picnic lunch, buy a round-trip ticket, Kandersteg to Adelboden. We suggest taking the 9:37 am train one stop from Kandersteg to Frutigen, arriving in time to take the 10:13 am bus outside the Frutigen train station. Arriving in Adelboden, turn right at the bus station, toward the center of town, and visit the Tourist Bureau, on the left side of the street, marked with the familiar "i." Locate the Hotel Kreuz, in the center of Adelboden, diagonally across from the "i", where a sign directs you to the Schwandfeldspitz Lift. Purchase a one-way ticket for this gondola ride, lifting *Easy Walkers* from 4,430 ft. to 6,400 ft. in 5 minutes. The view from the station offers a panorama of Adelboden, and an impressive view of the valley to the northeast, including Frutigen. A restaurant and facilities are available near the lift station.

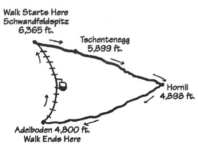

Walk Starts Here
Schwandfeldspitz
6,365 ft.

Tschentenegg
5,899 ft.

Hörnli
4,898 ft.

Adelboden 4,800 ft.
Walk Ends Here

Start: A sign outside the top lift station points to the right, "Tschentenegg - 15 minutes," "Hörnli - 50 minutes" and "Adelboden - 1 hour, 50 minutes." Walk to the right, up and over a small grassy meadow, following the trail down the ridge of the Tschentenegg. Proceed toward a small group of houses in the meadow in front of you. After walking about 20 minutes, ignore a sign indicating "Adelboden - 1 hour." Do not take this steep trail, but go straight ahead to "Hörnli - 30 minutes," "Adelboden - 1 hour." This is Tschentenegg at 5,675 ft., and within a short time you'll come to a split in the path, the left marked "Lechterweg" and the right marked "Steilerweg." "Steiler" means steep in German and while we have descended it carefully, we recommend the easier path to the left. Both forest trails lead to a small grassy plain, with the entire valley visible in front of you. The level of descent eases as you walk down on a path now marked not only with the familiar yellow diamond, but in rockier spots, with white-red-white blazes. Soon you'll reach an overlook with benches and yellow signs pointing to Adelboden.

Turn right and follow the sign marked, "Adelboden - 30 minutes, Unter Hörnli"—or the lower trail. This blazed path descends gently through the forest, eventually reaching the meadows and suburbs around Adelboden.

But take a moment as you get close to Adelboden. Look for an open garage on your left, with a bright orange arrow, housing some nice artwork and black and white photography. This small gallery is unattended, but cleverly put together, and worth a few minutes visit. As you go into the "gallery," lights will automatically turn on, and a well-organized display is presented on the walls. Each article is priced for sale and numbered, so that you may deposit the amount required in a cash box, and take your purchase with you. The artist even provides packaging material to protect the art as you travel on.

Within another 10 minutes you'll reach the bottom of the road, and a turn to the right brings you to the PTT bus station. Buses leave for Frutigen 15 minutes after the hour, for the picturesque bus ride, meeting the return train or bus to Kandersteg.

Walk #7:   Lauchernalp to Weissenreid to Blatten (through the Lötschental - Lötschen Valley)

   Walking Time - 3 hours

The little daily, handmade weather sign at the Kandersteg bahnhof ticket office showed a happy, sunny face in "die Lötschental"—The Lötschen Valley, while the weather in Kandersteg was marginal, with low, ominous clouds. What a great opportunity to go to the "other side." The Lötschbergbahn will take you through the tunnel to Goppenstein, to a waiting bus through the Lötschental to Wiler, and a cable car lift to Lauchernalp. You'll view the Lötschental from the top station, all the way to the Langgletscher.

This valley is divided by the quick flowing Lonza River, but more importantly, the valley appears to be lifted from another time in another century. The Lötschental was isolated for centuries, until roads and the Lötschberg Railway were built in the early 20th century. Each small village has managed to maintain most of the culture and character of the region, including many of the old, weatherbeaten, brown wooden barns—some in the traditional Valaisian "mazot" style. In fact, the new parts of the town are built in and around the landmark buildings. While some of the newer buildings are too modern for their setting, the valley has maintained a marvelous sense of historical significance.

We have departed from some of the more traditional trail walks in order to bring you by road, through these old mountain villages, filled with centuries old barns and homes.

The walk will begin at the top station, up and around on the Höhenweg, through meadow, forest and small alpine villages, to Tellialp, where *Easy Walkers* will take a mountain road through the charming old village of Weissenried. You will continue down to Blatten, another small village that has preserved its heritage, taking the bus back to Goppenstein, and the train to Kandersteg.

Directions: Today it's important to pack your picnic lunch, as most of the walking will be in remote alpine areas. Buy a round-trip ticket, Kandersteg, Goppenstein, Wiler, Lauchernalp, with the return from Blatten, via Goppenstein to Kandersteg. This ticket includes all fares including the lift from Wiler to Lauchenalp. Catch the 9:24 am train from Kandersteg, getting off in Goppenstein, the first stop after going through the Lötschberg Tunnel. Leave the station, following signs to the Lötschental bus. Take the bus outside the station marked "Lauchernalp," leaving at 9:42 am for the trip back in time. The bus enters the valley, reaching the lift station at Wiler where you catch the Lauchernalp cable car for the 5-minute ride to the top station. Just show your round-trip ticket to the attendant at the base station for entry to the cable car.

Start: The top station, at 6,562 ft., is actually at the foot of a small mountain village, with a ski school, sports store and many wooden chalets perched on the side of the mountain. Yellow signs direct you to the right to "Fafleralp - 2 hours, 30 minutes" on the "Lötschentaler Höhenweg." Look to the north to see the impressive Langgletscher, and the Lonza River flowing through the long, narrow valley below. Follow the signs towards Fafleralp, on a steadily ascending yellow-blazed mountain trail, as it turns around the side of the mountain, rising gently. The mountains and meadows are dotted with old, weathered, brown wooden barns, storing feed for the cows. You'll soon reach a high point of 6,760 ft., as the path begins to descend for the remainder of the walk. The trail continues to be unobstructed by trees, and in June and July, the blaze of color from the wild flowers is remarkable. The path goes through another mountain town called Weritzalp, narrowing here and taking on more of the "bergweg" character of a traditional mountain trail. Enter on to a shaded forest path, rocky at times, so watch your footing, and continue to descend along this yellow-blazed trail toward Fafleralp. The blazes turn red and white, alerting walkers to be more cautious, as you proceed to Tellialp, easily recognized by a small bridge and a rushing waterfall.

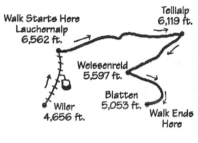

Walk Starts Here
Lauchernalp
6,562 ft.

Tellialp
6,119 ft.

Weissenreld
5,597 ft.

Blatten
5,053 ft.

Wiler
4,656 ft.

Walk Ends
Here

At Tellialp a sign indicates "Fafleralp" up to the left, or "Blatten" and "Reid," descending to the right on a comfortable wagon path. Proceed to Blatten down to the right, rejecting a path going down the mountain on a trail to your left, staying on the main wagon road, and eventually reaching Weissenried—the main reason we took you in this direction. Walk directly through this well-preserved tiny mountain village, with a small chapel originally built in the 1700s, surrounded by centuries-old weathered barns, some in disrepair, and others recently restored. We found this town to be a trip back in time, and loaded with photographic opportunities. Walking through Weissenried is like strolling through a small Swiss museum.

Follow signs to the picturesque village of Blatten, where you catch the bus back to Goppenstein, leaving 50 minutes past each hour. The bus to Goppenstein is timed to meet the return train to Kandersteg.

Today was spent walking through one of the most beautiful valleys in Switzerland, surrounded by high, snow-covered peaks and icy glaciers, with a tantalizing glimpse of the Switzerland that used to be—and still is, in many areas of the Lötschental!

Walk #8: Kandersteg to Frutigen

 Walking Time - 3 hours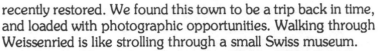

This low-level, 3-hour walk through the Kander Valley, could be reserved for a cloudy or rainy day. The walk proceeds north, past Blausee, descends easily through Inner Kandergrund, Kandergrund and Kanderbruche, eventually into Frutigen.

Options are provided, so if the weather turns **very** bad, there are several points along the path where a right turn brings you to a bus stop within a few minutes. You'll be walking from 3,850 ft., gently downhill to 2,625 ft., gradually descending through forest, meadow and farm communities, along the picturesque Kander River as it runs towards the Thunersee. After reaching Frutigen, you'll return to Kandersteg by train.

Start: Pack your picnic lunch as there are no restaurants on the trail during this 3-hour walk. Begin at the bahnhof, walking right as you face the station, through a parking lot, on to a path marked "Blausee" and "Frutigen." The entire walk is on a well-defined path, directing you towards Frutigen. Signs along the way point out Blausee (See Walk #2.) and various bus stops, if needed. Eventually the path becomes a small paved road, going through open meadows and the little villages of Inner Kandergrund, and Kandergrund, meeting a major auto road in Rybrugg. Follow signs to Kanderbruche and Frutigen by crossing the highway, making a right turn and then a quick left through a small parking lot, turning to follow along the Kander River to your left. This little path is marked with the yellow wanderweg diamond, and leads you towards a large house, but veers off to the left on a little grassy path, taking you in the direction of Frutigen, plainly visible as you walk north. The path leads into Kanderbruche, over the river, crossing the main road, and following the Wanderweg signs toward the church steeple of Frutigen, just over the major highway. Within a few minutes you'll be on the main street of the village, where a sign with the familiar "i" directs you up the hill to the Tourist Office. The bahnhof is to the right and any local street leads to the station.

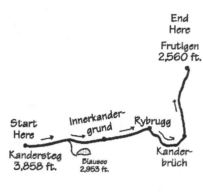

End
Here
Frutigen
2,560 ft.

Start
Here
Innerkander-
grund
Rybrugg
Kandersteg
3,858 ft.
Blausee
2,953 ft.
Kander-
brüch

Either the train or bus goes to Kandersteg, both leaving from the bahnhof. The train leaves 6 minutes after the hour, the bus leaves 47 minutes after the hour.

Walk #9:   Spiez to Spiezmoos to Einigen to Gwatt (excursion to Spiez Castle)

   Walking time: 3 1/2 hours

Our excursion and walk today can be taken if the weather in Kandersteg is overcast and not conducive to high-level walking. You will take the train to Spiez, and after walking around this little lakeside city, visit the famous Spiez museum and castle, overlooking Lake Thun. You will proceed on a low-level walk along the heights overlooking Lake Thun until reaching the little town of Spiezmoos, continuing to Einigen—mostly through shaded forest paths—to Gwatt, on the shores of Lake Thun.

The path is mostly downhill, except for an initial climb through the Spiez vineyards. Gwatt, Einigen and Spiez are all steamer stops on the Thunersee, presenting several options for the return trip—train, bus or lake steamer.

Spiez is a tranquil lakeside resort, built on a hillside, with the central part of the city located between the bahnhof and the lake. It offers museums, sailing, tennis and a lakeside castle with an old, Romanesque church. (See Excursion #1.)

Directions: Take the train to Spiez from Kandersteg, leaving 37 minutes after the hour, and within 1/2 hour you'll arrive

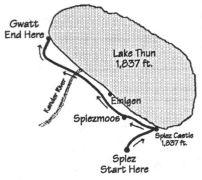

for the beginning of today's activities. After exiting the train station, turn right for a quick visit to the Tourist "i" Information Office, to pick up local maps of Spiez.

Start: Cross the street to a battery of yellow signs, including directions to "Gwatt - 2 hrs.," by way of "Spiezmoos" and "Einigen." As you look at beautiful blue Lake

Thun, you'll see prominent Spiez Castle, your first stop. Walk left, and within moments a sign directs you down the hill, in the direction of the lower part of the city and lake. Walk into a small business district, turning right at the second yellow pedestrian crossing, down the long street to the castle and the Thunersee. Toward the bottom of the hill, several steps on the left ascend directly to the castle.

After visiting the museum and castle, walk to the left of the building through an arch, and after some 100 yards on a cobblestoned path, a sign directs you right to, "Einigen-Gwatt - 1 hour 50 minutes." The lake is on the right, as you follow the path through the vineyards. After walking up through the grape arbors, turn right, following a green and white sign to "Spiezberg." This 30-minute walk is on a wide path through the forest, overlooking the Thunersee, ending in the heights above the suburb of Spiezmoos. When the path meets the road, turn right, entering a little town, with signs pointing in the direction of "Gwatt," down to the right. This path continues through the forest, not far from the lake shore, past Einigen, over the Kander River, through Gwattegg, eventually down to Gwatt.

There are several options for returning to Spiez from Gwatt—train, bus or lake steamer. **Note to *Easy Walkers*:** Bus and local train take you directly to the bahnhof for your return train trip to Kandersteg, while the steamer docks at the pier below the castle for a 15-minute walk up to the bahnhof.

SAMEDAN

We couldn't have made a better choice. Samedan is a lovely, quiet Engadine village, situated a stone's throw from its more famous sisters of St. Moritz and Pontresina, forming a central core for some of the world's best hiking. *Easy Walkers* might believe that the paths were put together specially for them, but walkers from all over Europe use these trails, enjoying the tranquility of the Swiss Engadine.

The well-preserved yet up-to-date village of Samedan appears to be a pop-up cutout from a colorful history book of Switzerland. The Engadine, in southeastern Switzerland, is probably the most interesting cultural and architectural area in the country. The Upper Engadine includes the famous resort towns of St. Moritz, Pontresina, Samedan and Zuoz, while the Lower Engadine is known for Zernez, Scuol and the Swiss National Park. Visitors to the Engadine, especially to the picturesque village of Zuoz, will marvel at the distinctively ornamented *sgraffito* houses, and the ancient Romansch language—sounding like a curious mix of Latin and Italian—spoken by about 80,000 residents of the area.

Samedan is situated at 5,900 ft., offering continuous rail and bus service, a small airport, and an 18-hole golf course, the oldest in Europe. The cost of accommodations in Samedan is somewhat less than St. Moritz and Pontresina, but it is just as close to the area's outstanding walking trails. Samedan has other attributes to recommend it—solitude, simplicity, understated elegance and a feeling of antiquity—all built upon century-old cobblestone streets.

There are dozens of high, medium and low paths and trails accessible from Samedan, connected by fast, inexpensive public transportation—either train or bus. To this we add the near perfect weather of southern Switzerland, more reliable in summer than other regions. Due to the popularity of the Engadine, reservations in any of these villages should be made well in advance.

Described are some of our favorite walks and excursions in the Samedan area, but there are many more waiting to be discovered by adventurous *Easy Walkers.*

Transportation

Zurich Airport to Samedan - After clearing Swiss Customs, follow the sign to the *Bahnhof*, marked with a symbol of a train. Stop at any ticket window to validate your Swiss Pass or Swiss Card. Take one of the frequent trains to Zurich Central, and change for the train to Chur, checking the large, overhead information panels for time and track number. In Chur, change trains for the 2-hour trip to Samedan.

Sample Timetable:

Zurich Airport to Zurich Central	**Take any train**
Zurich Central to Chur	**11:10 am dep**
Chur	**12:43 pm arr.**
Chur to Samedan	**13:03 pm arr. (1:03 pm)**
Samedan	**14:45 pm arr. (2:45 pm)**

Activities in Samedan

This section lists activities available in Samedan, when additions or alternatives to walking are desired. The Samedan Tourist Information office, telephone number 6 54 32, is on the main street, across from the Hotel Bellevue.

- Swimming
- Fishing
- 18-Hole Golf Course - the oldest in Switzerland. One-day greens fee is 80 SF, with reduced rates in June, September and October.
- Guided Excursions - to the Swiss National Park every Tuesday and Friday from the Tourist Office.
- Tennis - 16 SF/hour.

- Wildlife Observation Tour - in the Languard Valley every Thursday. Meet at the Tourist Office.
- Church Of San Peter - dates back to the 13th and 15th centuries. Follow the signs in town, up the hill.
- Chesa Planta - a Romansch library and museum, containing the cultural archives of the upper Engadine. Off the main street.
- Nature Trail - Muntarutsch to Selvas Plaunas to Proschimun to Planeg to Cristolais. Booklet with botanical information available at the "i."
- Par Cours - keep fit trail.

Excursions in and Around Samedan

This section introduces day excursions for *Easy Walkers* to enjoy when the weather is not suitable for high-altitude walking, or if an alternative to walking is desired. Be sure to check local timetables for best connections if using public transportation.

1. St. Moritz - The touristy, year-round resort of St. Moritz is a short, 10-minute train ride from Samedan. Situated at 6,000 ft. in a unique landscape of crystal-clear lakes, fragrant pine woods, imposing glaciers and majestic mountains, St. Moritz also boasts a long tradition as a spa town.

The St. Moritz Tourist "i" Office, is located at via Maistra 12, in the main square past Hanselman's Tea Room, for additional information about:

- a) Chesa Veglia - an old Engadine House
- b) Druiden Stone - site of the first settlers of the Engadine
- c) Church of San Gian - 11th- and 12th-century frescoes
- d) Olympic Stone - monument to the Olympic gold medal winners of 1928 and 1948
- e) Leaning Tower - the only remains of the original village built in 1193
- f) Segantini Museum - paintings by well-known local artist
- g) Engadine Museum - collection of rooms furnished in the local style with outstanding examples of sgraffito.

St. Moritz is the home of four world-famous trains: the incomparable Glacier Express to Zermatt, Engadin Express to Salzburg and Vienna, Palm Express to Ascona, Lugano and Italy, and Bernina Express to Italy.

St. Moritz is also the site of four aerial cableways:

a) Sessellift (chairlift) Suvretta to Randolins at 7,260 ft.

b) Luftseilbahn (cable car) St. Moritz Bad to Signal at 7,160 ft.

c) Drahtseilbahn (funicular railway) St. Moritz Dorf to Chantarella to Corviglia - at 8,160 ft.

d) Luftseilbahn (cable car) Corviglia to Piz Nair - at 10,030 ft.

Directions to St. Moritz: Trains run approximately every half-hour from the Samedan station to St. Moritz, and return. Buses also go to St. Moritz—get off at Schoolhouse Platz stop—in the heart of the shopping area. A city bus runs between St. Moritz *Bad,* the spa area, and St. Moritz *Dorf,* the main shopping and hotel area.

2. Pontresina - Six miles east of St. Moritz, at an altitude of 6,000 ft., Pontresina lies on a high, sunny terrace, surrounded by the snow-capped peaks of the Bernina mountains, and is a favorite destination of hikers from around the world.

The Alp Languard chair lift rises above Pontresina, to 7,450 ft.—the start of many walks (See Walk #4.)—providing incredible views into the Roseg Valley.

A popular excursion from Pontresina is the *Pferde Omnibus,* or horse-drawn carriage, taking visitors on a delightful one-hour ride into the Roseg Valley to the Hotel Roseggletscher with its famous dessert buffet. Call Luigi Costa at 6 60 57 for reservations, and pick up the horse and wagon a few minutes walk from the Pontresina railroad station. (See Walk #1.)

Directions to Pontresina: Trains to Pontresina leave Samedan every 30 to 40 minutes, and return to Samedan at 1 minute and 31 minutes past every hour.

3. Zuoz - Considered the best preserved village in the Upper Engadine, Zuoz nestles at 5,750 ft. in lush green meadows. The village has retained its original character—restoring the elegant 16th- and 17th-century decorated houses. In fact, most of the 1,200 inhabitants speak Romansch as well as German. Photographic opportunities abound, and *Easy Walkers* will enjoy wandering through the cobblestone streets and narrow alleys.

Directions to Zuoz: Trains leave Samedan for Zuoz at 8:55 am and 10:12 am, for a 15-minute ride, and return at 49 minutes after every hour.

4. Celerina - Lying between St. Moritz and Samedan, this Engadine village of only 850 is sometimes considered a suburb of glitzier St. Moritz. Celerina contains charming, Engadine houses, worth exploring on a walk from Samedan. (See Walk #6.) One-third mile east of town, the old Romanesque church of San Gian stands alone on a hill—investigate its painted ceiling and remains of frescoes dating from 1478.

The famous Cresta ski run from St. Moritz, ends in Celerina, near the large, old hotels.

The gondola from Celerina to Marguns takes walkers to 7,475 ft., and the chairlift from Marguns to Corviglia rises to 8,160 ft., with an even more spectacular view of the Upper Engadine.

Directions to Celerina: Trains run every half hour between Samedan and Celerina, on the St. Moritz line, for a 4-minute trip. The PTT bus, leaving every hour, also takes 4 minutes.

5. Sils-Maria and Sils-Baselgia - With a combined population of less than 500, these quiet, yet charming resorts in the Upper Engadine are situated at the beginning of the En (Inn) Valley. From 1881 to 1889, Sils-Maria was summer home to the philosopher Nietzsche—the museum is to the right of the main PTT station.

The Furtschellas aerial cable car ascends to 7,585 ft., for a view of the Upper Engadine region, its glittering lakes, snow-covered mountains and icy glaciers. The Pferde Omnibus leaves every day from the Post Office in Sils Maria for trips into the beautiful Fex Valley. Reservations are necessary—call 4 52 86.

Directions to Sils: From Samedan, take the 9:12 am train, arriving in St. Moritz at 9:20 am. The 9:35 PTT bus to Sils Maria is in front of the St. Moritz train station, arriving at 10:01. To return to Samedan from Sils, buses leave at 22 and 48 minutes. past the hour. Change buses at Schoolhouse Platz in St. Moritz for the bus to Samedan through Celerina.

6. Scuol - Tarasp - Vulpera - This trio of neighboring Lower Engadine villages boast mineral springs reputedly beneficial to sufferers of liver and kidney ailments. We can't attest to the efficacy of these cures, but these tiny towns, with their cobblestone streets and sgraffito houses, are enchanting. A bus from Scuol or Tarasp takes you to Schloss Tarasp, a castle restored in the early 1900s and still used occasionally by the Prince of Hesse-Darmstadt.

Directions to Scuol: Trains leave Samedan regularly for the 1 1/4-hour ride to Scuol. The 10:12 am train arrives in Scuol at 11:28 am. Return trains to Samedan leave Scuol at 50 minutes past each hour.

7. Poschiavo - This small, Italian-speaking village, accessible by train through the Bernina Pass, offers a different style of architecture and surroundings from its Engadine neighbors—attractively mixing German and Italian styles into its transalpine surroundings. From July 1 through September 1, an open-air market is held every Wednesday in the town square. Check with the Samedan Tourist Office for details.

Directions to Poschiavo: The 10:07 am train from Samedan (change in Pontresina) arrives in Poschiavo at 11:40 am. To return, the 4:20 pm train arrives in Samedan at 6:08 pm (change in Pontresina).

8. Swiss National Park - This alpine sanctuary is protected so plants and animals are allowed to develop without human interference. Please use only marked paths, take out any refuse and don't pick flowers or disturb animals. The National Park House is in Zernez, and we recommend a stop before entering the park. You'll be informed about exhibitions and receive current information on walking trails.

Directions to Zernez and the Swiss National Park: The 10:12 am train from Samedan arrives in Zernez at 10:53, and the 4:25 train from Zernez returns to Samedan at 5:05pm.

9. Diavolezza -   An 11-minute cable ride to 9,764 ft., Diavolezza offers a spectacular glacial panorama.

Directions to Diavolezza: Take the train from Samedan to Pontresina and change for the train to Poschiavo, exiting at the Bernina-Diavolezza station—a 23-minute ride from Pontresina. Return to Samedan by changing trains in Pontresina.

10. Piz Lagalb - The view from 9,512 ft. at Piz Lagalb encompasses 40 of the high, surrounding peaks, including Diavolezza and its glaciers. An incredible variety of alpine flowers grow on the slopes of this mountain, and marmots and ibex can still be seen. Because this cable car is only a few minutes train ride from Diavolezza, plan the day to visit both peaks. Restaurants and facilities are at the top stations of each.

Directions to Piz Lagalb: Take the train to Pontresina and change for the train to Poschiavo, exiting at the Bernina Lagalb station, a few minutes after the Diavolezza stop. Return to Samedan by changing trains in Pontresina.

11. Chur - Although this city of 30,000 inhabitants is a large trade center, *Easy Walkers* will enjoy exploring its extensive old town. The narrow, cobblestoned, colorful streets are bordered by old houses, towers and squares decorated with fountains, flowers and flags. Be sure to visit the Kathedrale, built in the 12th and 13 centuries, remodelled in 1811 after a fire. Inside, notice the 15th-century Gothic triptych at the altar—the largest in Switzerland. The "i" (follow the signs outside the train station) can provide walking maps of the old town area.

Directions to Chur: Take the narrow-gauge Rhätische Bahn Railroad from Samedan and Chur—an exciting, scenic trip of two hours each way.

Samedan Walks

Walk #1: Pontresina to Val Roseg to Pontresina (excursion to Pontresina)

Walking Time - 2-4 hours

This particularly lovely valley walk will take *Easy Walkers* from Pontresina, gently up on a forest path, to the foot of the Val Roseg Glacier. The path ascends easily and in two hours you'll reach the Restaurant Roseggletscher, with a most delectable pastry buffet served on the sun-terrace—you'll feel you've arrived at dessert-heaven! Picnic in the surrounding meadows or by the river, and gaze at the wonders of the glacier.

Easy Walkers can return to Pontresina on the same path, or take the 50-minute *Pferde Omnibus* (horse and wagon ride) back to Pontresina—cost: 11 SF. Make reservations for this wagon ride in advance, either going or returning. Call Luigi Costa at 6 60 57. These wagons are open, seat about 10 people, and provide new perspectives of the Roseg Valley.

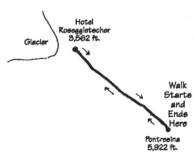

After returning to Pontresina, a walk up the hill will bring you to the town center, filled with shops, hotels and a selection of outdoor cafes. The Tourist Office, marked with a big "i," is across from the Post Hotel.

Today's walk takes you gradually from 5,922 ft. to 6,562 ft. The terrain is mixed, with a few mountain trails, both wide and narrow, but usually with other walkers. The path is well-signed and well-defined, with no chance for confusion—this is one of the most popular walks in the Pontresina area.

Directions: Pick up your picnic lunch in Samedan and purchase a round-trip train ticket, Samedan to Pontresina. We suggest taking the 9:10 am train, and within 10 minutes you'll be at the bahnhof at Pontresina.

Start: Leaving the station, turn right, and circle up the hill in the direction of Pontresina. A sign directs you to "The Val Roseg Wagon Ride-150 m." If you choose to take the horse and wagon going up to the glacier, this is where you board the wagon. To walk into the valley, continue up the hill, and within a few minutes you'll see a yellow sign, "Val Roseg Footpath." This sign is on your right, in front of a parking lot, with the path beginning in back of the lot, going slightly up to the right. Shortly, another sign will direct you left, "Val Roseg-2 hrs." Stay on the main, marked trail. The path begins to ascend easily. As you progress on this shaded forest trail, the impressive Inn River is on the right. Within 30 minutes, the snow-capped peaks of the Roseg range appear above the pine trees, wild flowers blooming on all sides of this well-defined trail. This path is also used by mountain bikers, so it's a good idea to stay to the right most of the time.

When the path touches the river, photographers will appreciate the rushing waterfalls of the Inn River, framed by the nearby pine trees and the towering, snow-capped peaks above the glacier.

The path meets the road, but we recommend taking the trail left, through the forest. About 20 minutes from the hotel, the path joins the road, then takes you right, over a small bridge where the restaurant and glacier are in full view. Walk through the flocks of geese, around to the sun-terrace in back of the hotel to a picnic bench just above the terrace. Don't forget to check out the famous dessert buffet on the terrace—there are no less than 30 varieties of homemade kuchen, pies, cakes and fresh fruit. We'll leave the rest up to you!

After lunch, a walk around the restaurant will disclose many signs directing hikers to various destinations. Before taking any additional walks, make your decision: take that wonderful horse and wagon ride to Pontresina, or walk back in the same manner you came. If you decide to take the wagon, make arrangements with one of the many available carriagemen, if you didn't do so earlier. The wagon ride is 50 minutes, while the return walk will take about 1 3/4 hours. Now you can determine how much time you want to spend *spaziering* (walking) towards the Roseg Glacier. One of the paths takes you to Alp Ota in one hour—a trail close to the glacier. Another path takes you to Tschierva, at 8,563 ft., in 1 3/4 hours. Or, you might pick any path, walk through the valley near the glacier, and return when you feel it's time to take the wagon ride or walk back to Pontresina.

Once you've finished walking, or stepped down from the wagon in Pontresina, a right turn brings you into Pontresina for sightseeing or shopping. A left turn takes you to the bahnhof, where trains run every hour, on the hour, back to Samedan.

Walk #2: Sils Baselgia to Grevasalvas to Sils Maria (excursions to Sils Maria and St. Moritz)

 Walking Time - 3 hours

Do you remember the movie *Heidi?* Today's walk is to the tiny alpine settlement where *Heidi* was filmed. *Easy Walkers* will take the train to St. Moritz and change for the bus to Sils Baselgia, where the trail begins. This high-level, mountain walk to Grevasalvas is on a path offering unparalleled views of the Lej de Segl. After a steady climb from 5,900 to 6,560 ft., you'll reach the heights overlooking Grevasalvas. We're not sure Grandfather is around any more, but this wondrous little town is still situated on its grassy alp, surrounded by grazing cows and craggy peaks. After conjuring up fascinating images of blonde braids, dirndl skirts and gentle, pipe-smoking grandpas, you'll return on the same path, as you proceed down the mountain towards Sils-Baselgia, Sils-Maria and St. Moritz.

Directions: It's important to bring a picnic lunch today, as you'll be up on the mountain at lunch time with no restaurants available. Bear in mind also—there are no facilities for the entire length of this walk, but of course, you always stow important accessories in your back pack for emergencies. Buy a round trip-ticket at the railroad station, Samedan to Sils-Baselgia. We suggest taking the 9:12 am train to St. Moritz, arriving at 9:20 am. Take the 9:35 am bus to Sils-Baselgia, outside the front of the station and to the left. This pleasant, 35-minute ride through the valley, makes short stops at the pretty towns of Champfer, Silvaplana, Surlej and Sils-Maria.

Start: When you get off the bus, walk straight ahead, through the small village of Sils-Baselgia, toward the mountains. After crossing the highway carefully, a sign directs you left, up a mountain path towards Grevasalvas. This stone-strewn path is shaded by a pine forest, and ascends 650 ft., gradually and comfortably. Crossing streams and old rock slides, it's important to note again that consistent pace is more important than speed. Set a pace that is comfortable, and try to maintain it. Of course, as ascents become steeper, you'll walk slower to meet your individual needs.

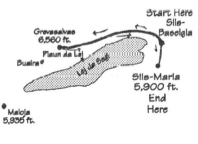

A sign directs you to "Grevasalvas - 1/2 hr.," with waterfalls on the right, as you step over streams, ascending a bit more steeply, on a narrow, rocky, but well-defined trail. You'll reach the high point of 6,562 ft., and the tiny town of Grevasalvas is below and to the left. You can either walk down a steep path to this hamlet of a dozen houses, or stay on the hillside and enjoy a picnic lunch. This green-carpeted alp sits in the midst of high, barren, craggy peaks, leaving us wondering how they filmed *Heidi*

at Grevasalvas—a miniscule, remote Swiss village that is perhaps duplicated hundreds of times in regions throughout the Swiss Alps.

After lunch, several options can be taken to return. We prefer retracing our steps, and spending time in Sils-Maria, taking the bus back to visit St. Moritz later in the afternoon. If you choose a different route, walk past Grevasalvas, through Buaira, the tiny town visible in the distance about half a mile past Grevasalvas, following the signs to Maloja. This route brings you from 6,562 to 5,955 ft. in about 1 1/2 hours. Buses leave regularly from Maloja to St. Moritz, where you change at Schoolhouse Platz for the bus to Samedan.

When asked, "Why take the same route back?", we reply, "To achieve new perspectives by walking in the opposite direction." This reverse walk back to Sils-Baselgia is mostly downhill, and should take about 1 1/4 hours. At the base of the trail, cross the road, past a restaurant with sun-terrace and facilities. Continue to walk up the main street into Sils-Maria (see Excursion #3.), where the bus takes you to St. Moritz Schoolhouse Platz stop. This bus stop is in the heart of the St. Moritz shopping area (see Excursion #1.), and a short block from the famous Hanselman's tea room and pastry shop, with some of the most mouth-watering desserts in town. Check the bus schedule back to Samedan from Schoolhouse Platz before exploring St. Moritz.

Today's trip is a challenging day of mountain walking, well within the capability of *Easy Walkers*. In fact, this walk was suggested to us by a couple in their 80s, both physicians, whom we met hiking from Zermatt to Zmutt.

Walk #3:   Zuoz to Madulain to La Punt to Bever to Samedan (excursion to Zuoz)

   Walking Time - 3 hours

Zuoz nestles in lush green meadows at 5,742 ft., far from the hustle and bustle of St. Moritz, and is considered to be the best preserved village in the Upper Engadine. Today's excursion and walk brings *Easy Walkers* to Zuoz, leaving time to visit, photograph and have lunch. The afternoon will be made up of a level walk through the valley from Zuoz to the small, but photogenic villages of Madulain, La Punt and Bever—largely through the meadows and close to the Inn River. The Engadine is dominated by magnificent, patrician houses, originally built in the 16th and 17th century. Although refurbished and renovated, they retain their original and unique character, decorated with beautiful flowers and unique sgraffito.

The meadows are covered with wild flowers, mostly dried by mid-August, but filled with cows grazing in the pastures. Photographers will find this valley offers exceptional opportunities—as autumn approaches, the Engadine takes on new colors, with the nearby woods offering a unique contrast to the clear blue sky.

Zuoz, serviced by bus and rail, is only 15 minutes by train from Samedan, and has over 120 miles of hiking paths, from difficult mountain bergwegs to gentle valley wanderwegs.

Directions: Purchase a one-way ticket, Samedan to Zuoz and take the 10:12 am train, arriving at 10:28 am. Cross the tracks carefully at this little station and walk up the hill to the town center. As you reach the main street, make a right turn, and within a few minutes the town square appears, in the shadow of the church steeple. Take an hour or so to explore the cobblestoned streets and alleys before beginning today's walk. If you haven't brought a picnic lunch, there are several restaurants with outdoor terraces and facilities.

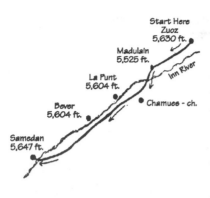

Start Here
Zuoz
5,630 ft.

Madulain
5,525 ft.

La Punt
5,604 ft.

Inn River

Bever
5,604 ft.

Chamues - ch.

Samedan
5,647 ft.

Start: Leave the village by retracing your steps to the railroad station. At the station, make a right turn, walk through the long parking lot to the end, and pick up a path through a small tunnel underneath the railroad tracks. Walk past the Restaurant Dorta, down to the river. Turn right, following the sign to Madulain along the river path. There are several other paths in the direction of Samedan, but we prefer this one because it takes *Easy Walkers* through another tiny, quiet, charming, well-preserved and very special Engadine village—Madulain. After 15 minutes of walking on a cart path along the river, note the small town of Champesch on the hillside to the right. In another 10 minutes the path veers up a hill to the right, where a sign points left to Madulain. This is the Zuoz-Madulain Innweg, a promenade walk between the two villages along the Inn River. As you proceed, Madulain comes into full view, and in the distance to the left is Chamuesch-ch. Walk ahead through Madulain on its main road, noticing the very special quality of this tiny Engadine village. As you leave, the path crosses a major auto road, but take the little wooden bridge over the river on your left. Make a sharp right turn at the end of the bridge, down a flight of plank stairs, under the auto road, with the path spilling into the meadow on the other side. Continue to a four-way intersection, taking the path to the right to La Punt-Bever.

La Punt lies directly ahead, and you'll soon be at the main road. At the Hotel Krone, you have the option of turning right and following the signs to the station, or *stazione,* to catch the next train back to Samedan.

To continue the walk, cross the street behind the Hotel Krone to follow directions to Bever-Samedan-Pontresina. A small wooden bridge crosses a stream to a path alongside the river. The walk to Bever puts the Inn River on your right. If you wish, you can follow the sign to Bever and visit this village by crossing the river and auto road, continuing your walk to Samedan from the center of town—or stay on the path directly into Samedan.

Walk #4:   Alp Languard to Pontresina

Walking Time - 3 1/2 hours

The mountains towering over Pontresina, St. Moritz and neighboring villages, are the setting for today's walk—on a well-defined path, with stunning views of the Val Roseg (Roseg Valley) and its glacier. The return path descends on a trail that zigzags through the forest and meadows filled with colorful flowers framed against distant snow-capped peaks. The walk brings you down from 7,546 ft. to 5,905 ft., and there is ample time to visit the picturesque town of Pontresina before returning to the train station for the quick trip to Samedan.

Directions: Trains leave from Samedan station to Pontresina, every 1/2 hour, and after picking up your picnic provisions, purchase a round-trip ticket. Turn right, outside the Pontresina station and walk in the direction of Pontresina. As you proceed up the hill, a large yellow sign on a fence directs you a bit further to the Alp Languard lift. You'll arrive at the main street in Pontresina, opposite the local Tourist Office, with its blue and white "i" information sign. Maps, information, weather conditions, etc., are available, and when ready to leave, continue up the hill for about 100 ft. to the Alp Languard chairlift. Purchase a one-way ticket to the top, and within 15 minutes you'll arrive via a double-seat, open chairlift. **Note to *Easy Walkers*: before getting on the lift, remove your backpack so you can settle into the lift chair safely, with your backpack on your lap, as the overhead bar drops into place.**

Start: At the top, follow the sign pointing right and down the hill on the "Hoheweg-Muottas Muragl-2 1/2 hrs." A few minutes spent at this point is worthwhile, as you observe many walkers—some on the high mountain trail up to the 10,500 ft. peak Languard, others walking down one of several steep trails through the forest to Pontresina, while still others will move up the mountain to the Segantinihütte.

As you pass a restaurant, a group of signs will send you left, once again, to "Muottas Muragl-2 1/2 hrs.," on a well-defined trail. Pontresina and its large, grand old hotels, are in full view in the valley to the left.

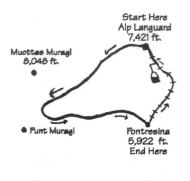

Start Here
Alp Languard
7,421 ft.

Muottas Muragl
8,048 ft.

Punt Muragl

Pontresina
5,922 ft.
End Here

St. Moritz makes its appearance in the distance, surrounded by snow-capped mountains, with beautiful blue lakes extending through the valley to Sils. Wild flowers are ablaze with color up on the mountain and down the rocky slopes to the left, more pronounced in early summer, drying as fall approaches. After about an hour you'll reach a sign pointing to the left path, and a large red and white Swiss flag announcing a restaurant with sun-terrace and facilities. However, proceed on the right path towards Muottas Muragl. Continuing on this main trail, you'll reach a point where a panoramic wonderland comes into view: to the left, Val Roseg and its formidable glacier; ahead, St. Moritz and a chain of lakes; and far to your right, the little villages of Celerina and Samedan. The view is so impressive it's worth a rest and photography stop to absorb the beauty. Walkers will continue to pass you in both directions, all smitten with the view—and it's a good spot for a picnic.

Shortly, as you gently ascend, a group of signs offers some tions:

1. Continue up to Muottas Muragl, which can plainly be seen in front of you, with a cable car descent down to the train at Punt Muragl, taking you back to Samedan.

2. Return on the same path, reversing direction, back to Alp Languard, with fresh new views, taking the chairlift back down to Pontresina, the same way you came up earlier today.

3. Turn left and follow the sign to Pontresina, on a descending, well-defined trail, through forest and meadow. The return walk to Pontresina will take 1 3/4 hours, and we recommend this option to *Easy Walkers*. You will also see a sign to Samedan, but we suggest that you do not follow that particular path.

The trail to Pontresina initially zigzags down the mountain, and while steep in some places, is comfortable and safe—in fact most Europeans begin at the base and walk up the path you are now descending. Buttonhooking left and right to cut the angle of descent adds to the beauty of the walk, as your views constantly change.

Reminder to *Easy Walkers*: walking downhill can cause stress to the knees and toes, take your time, rest often. Continuing down the mountain, the angle of descent eases considerably and the trail becomes very comfortable.

A final sign indicates "Pontresina-10 min." and the path meets a paved road, approaching the suburbs of Pontresina. At the first intersection, a sign to "Pontresina-Laret" directs you to the right. At the small sign "Menqiots," take a left, continuing down to the main street of Pontresina. Turn left, passing a large, castle-like hotel, now a Club Med. Turn right at the Bahnhof sign and walk back to the train station, or walk straight ahead and visit Pontresina, its shops, hotels and restaurants. The train to Samedan leaves on each hour.

Walk #5: St. Moritz to Surlej to Corvatschbahn to Murtel to Fuorcla Surlej to Murtel (excursion to Corvatsch)

 Walking Time - 2-4 hours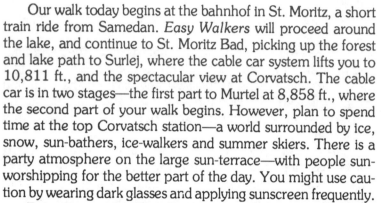

Our walk today begins at the bahnhof in St. Moritz, a short train ride from Samedan. *Easy Walkers* will proceed around the lake, and continue to St. Moritz Bad, picking up the forest and lake path to Surlej, where the cable car system lifts you to 10,811 ft., and the spectacular view at Corvatsch. The cable car is in two stages—the first part to Murtel at 8,858 ft., where the second part of your walk begins. However, plan to spend time at the top Corvatsch station—a world surrounded by ice, snow, sun-bathers, ice-walkers and summer skiers. There is a party atmosphere on the large sun-terrace—with people sun-worshipping for the better part of the day. You might use caution by wearing dark glasses and applying sunscreen frequently.

Returning to the Murtel station, you'll begin the walk to Fuorcla Surlej and its views of the Val Roseg. A cable car descent to the base station brings you to the bus to St. Moritz for the return to Samedan.

Directions: Pick up your picnic lunch and proceed to the railroad station, buying a one-way ticket, Samedan to St. Moritz.

Start: When you arrive at the St. Moritz bahnhof, walk down the stairs as if you were exiting, but at the bottom of the stairs, turn in the direction of Track #6, emerging on the other side of the station. Cross over a small bridge and pick up the path around the lake, walking along the lake with the elegant, old Hotel Waldhaus on your left and the lake on your right. This paved path eventually becomes a wide, comfortable dirt path on the shady side of the lake. St. Moritz-Dorf, the main shopping area, is in full view across the lake to the right. In 45 minutes you'll reach St. Moritz Bad, with its famous spas. Make

a right turn on to the city street, walking through a main shopping area of St. Moritz-Bad,

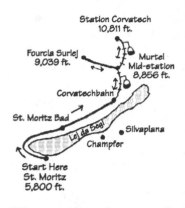

following signs to the tourist
office. Proceed through a
park area towards the "i", located in a major hotel and
spa, directly ahead and slightly to the left. Inside the lobby
you'll notice people "taking
the waters," filling canteens
and bottles—take a few
minutes to sample the
mineral water from the large
fountain.

When ready to leave, walk through the parking lot to the
back, up the hill and to the right, following signs pointing in the
direction of "Champfer - 45 min." and "Surlej - 1 hr." This is
a comfortable, shaded forest path, well-used by bikers and
walkers, so be a little cautious and stay on the right side of the
path. Pass through a crossroads and a sign pointing ahead to
"Champfer - 35 min." and "Surlej - 50 min." While still on this
meadow path, you might see future young olympic athletes in
training for a variety of winter sports. This particular area is
used extensively by Swiss coaches for training speed skaters
and cross-country skiers. The day we walked by, young athletes
were preparing for the 1994 olympics.

Walking through a campground, the path turns into a small
paved auto road. Proceed up the hill and signs direct you to
"Champfer-25 min." At the top of the hill on your left is the
famous St. Moritz olympic ski jump. The road continues straight
ahead on the right side of the tennis courts, and within a few
minutes the lake itself appears. Proceed left, walking along the
shaded part of the lake, away from the road, in a westerly direction. Stay on the trail closest to the water, as bikers use the
wider path.

After you have walked about 1 1/2 hours the town of Silvaplana appears on the right, the lift to Corvatsch on the left.
At the main road, turn left, walk past the PTT bus stop, follow-

ing the signs through the little village of Surlej, up to the lift station, about a 1/2-hour walk.

Purchase a round-trip ticket to Corvatsch and take the 2-stage cable car. At the Murtel mid-station, transfer immediately to the second stage. As you arrive at the 10,000 ft. top station, walk slowly until your body adjusts to the altitude. The panorama in every direction is incredible—from the Maloja Pass on the left, past St. Moritz on the right—mountains, glaciers and snow, to lakes, meadows and tiny Engadine villages.

At this point, *Easy Walkers* have two options:

1. Return to Samedan by way of the Corvatschbahn and PTT bus.

2. Continue the walk from the Murtel middle station to Fuorcla Surlej and back—another 2 hours—and then returning to Samedan by way of the Corvatschbahn and bus.

Take the cable car down to the middle station to begin the second stage of the walk. Murtel is at 8,865 ft., and as you emerge from the cable car, notice a group of signs directing you to "Fuorcla Surlej - 40 min." You'll be walking over mixed terrain, through fairly barren landscape above the tree line, arriving at Fuorcla Surlej before the hour is up. Plan another hour for the walk back to Murtel.

To return to Samedan, take the gondola down to the base station and catch the bus to St. Moritz, leaving 58 minutes past each hour. Do not get off at the St. Moritz Bahnhof to take the train to Samedan, continue on the bus to the last St. Moritz stop at Schoolhouse Platz, and change to another bus for the short ride to Samedan through Celerina, riding past the famous St. Moritz Cresta ski run.

Walk #6: Ospizio Bernina to Sassal Massone to Alp Grum

Walking Time - 2 1/2 hours

The area of Switzerland closest to the Dolomites that separate Italy from Switzerland, provides the setting for today's walk. All of the walking will be in the open, on and around mountains that are bare, craggy and rocky—almost like walking on the moon. You will take the train to the little station of Ospizio Bernina, where the walk begins, and hike in an easy ascent from 7,218 ft. to Sassal Massone, a restaurant at 7,727 ft.

The views of beautiful Lake Bianco and the nearby glacier, dominate the panorama. The walk continues down the mountain to the 6,680 ft. railroad station at Alp Grum, for the train ride back to Samedan. This walk takes place near the famous Bernina Pass, and you may catch a glimpse of the world-renowned Bernina Express as it makes its way through southeastern Switzerland.

The train from Samedan to Ospizio Bernina has brought you to the Italian-influenced region of Switzerland, and the signs and names are now in Italian, instead of German or Romansch. This change in atmosphere makes Switzerland even more appealing to visitors, as language, customs, cuisine, dress and living styles change dramatically the closer you get to the Italian border—*see* or lake, becomes *lago,* and *stunde* or hour, is now *ora.*

Directions: Pick up your picnic lunch, and purchase a ticket from Samedan to Ospizio Bernina, with a return from Alp

Grum to Samedan. We suggest taking the 9:10 am train to Pontresina, and changing for the train to Ospizio Bernina and Tirano. That train will be waiting on an adjacent platform. Sit on the right side for the best views on your trip, and within the hour you'll be at your destination—Ospizio Bernina.

Start: At the end of the station, a sign directs you ahead to "Alp Grum - 1 hr.," and "Sassal Massone - 1 1/4 hrs." Walk along the lake and railroad tracks, on a blazed white-red-white path. As you come to the end of the lake, the road forks. Take either path for a short distance till you come to another fork in the road and a sign indicating, "Sassal Massone," to the right. The left path stays lower and goes directly to the Alp Grum station. Proceeding up the mountain, the elevation increases from 7,330 ft. to 7,727 ft., bringing *Easy Walkers* to the Sassal Massone restaurant, near the foot of the glacier.

While the restaurant has a large sun-terrace and facilities, why not choose a rock on the nearby hillside for a picnic lunch. The view from this point is outstanding, but when the moment beckons, walk to the rear of the sun-terrace, down a rocky dirt path facing the glacier. This trail can be described as a rocky, narrow, mountain *bergweg,* but it is well-marked, well-defined and well-used. There are many little side trails, but we encourage *Easy Walkers* to stay on the main path, marked white-red-white. The trail buttonhooks and instead of facing the glacier, turns towards the small train station of Alp Grum. Again we remind you that downhill walking can bring stress to knees and toes. **Tighten those laces and rest as needed.** Walking here in September was a delight—the sun was hot but the breezes at 8,500 ft. were cool and comfortable.

Within an hour you'll reach the bottom of the mountain. Turn right on a path up to the railroad tracks, and follow a sign pointing to a lower path along the tracks for the 10-minute walk to Alp Grum station and its restaurant, pretty sun-terrace and facilities. Trains back to Pontresina and Samedan run every hour.

Walk #7: Samedan to Celerina to Pontresina to Samedan (excursion to Alp Languard in Pontresina)

 Walking Time: 3 1/2 hours

This low-level walk takes *Easy Walkers* through the valley from Samedan to Celerina for a visit and continues on to Pontresina, returning to Samedan along the side of the golf course that lies just outside the village.

This walk is fairly level and should be used on the day before, or the day after a high-level walk—to help keep your walking interesting—and your knees and feet in good shape.

Start: There are several trails from Samedan to Celerina. Since we promised a low-level day, walk down the hill from the Hotel des Alpes, crossing the railroad tracks, to the bridge over

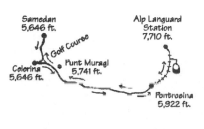

the Inn River, where a sign directs you to the right, before crossing the bridge, to "Celerina - 45 min." Proceeding on this level path, the river will be on the left, and shortly the path continues to the right as the river forks. Walk into Celerina, and when ready to leave, follow the auto road back down to the river, making a right turn just before you reach the river. You will

be continuing on the same path and in the same direction as this morning. The well-signed path goes along the meadow, with the auto road to the distant left, adjacent to the railroad tracks—finally taking you into a large parking lot at the Pontresina railroad station. Continue to walk past the station and follow the road as it turns left and goes up the hill.

Pontresina is set at the base of a mountain, somewhat up from the station. The street curves to the left, meeting the main shopping street of Pontresina. A right turn on the main street brings you to the information office, marked with an "i," where you can pick up brochures about local events, including sports, concerts, special excursions, cable car information and other walks in the area.

If you are not planning to take Walk #4, this is a good time for an excursion to Alp Languard. Leaving the information office, turn left, continuing up and around the road for approximately 100 ft. to the lift station, and purchase a round-trip ticket to Alp Languard at 7,422 ft. This is a double chairlift and fun, as you are automatically shifted from one lift system to a second lift system, somewhat like a tame ride at an amusement park. The incredible views from this station include Diavolezza to the left at 9,771 ft., straight ahead to the Val Roseg and its famous glacier, and the St. Moritz valley on the right.

Take the chairlift down to the base station for your walk to Samedan. Follow the road down through Pontresina to the railroad station, make a right turn and walk through the parking lot, following directions to Punt Muragl. Turn left through the underpass, where a sign points to Punt Muragl. This is a level walk through the meadows, with the river on your right. At a fork in the road, go straight ahead on the lower path, and soon you'll come to an auto road with a sign directing you to Celerina to the left and Samedan to the right. Turn right over the bridge, and quickly to the left, continuing your walk on the right side of the river. This is a pretty walk, nice and breezy in the afternoon, the golf course on the right, as you continue along the river. In 45 minutes you'll be back in Samedan. Turn left over the bridge and railroad tracks to your hotel.

OTHER GREAT WALKING EASY AREAS IN SWITZERLAND

Switzerland has hundreds of charming villages and thousands of great walking trails, but we couldn't possibly include them all. Here is a list of a few areas we visited and enjoyed, but couldn't cover in detail because of space limitations.

1. Arosa - a special train takes *Easy Walkers*, via mountain ridges, sky-high trestles, alpine meadows and tiny mountain villages, to the internationally famous ski resort of Arosa. The main part of Arosa, at 5,740 ft., is built on the heights around two small lakes, and most of the hotels have views overlooking the lakes and adjacent mountains. While the architecture of the hotels and homes doesn't equal some of the quainter areas of Switzerland, Arosa offers a great variety of activities and an abundance of walking trails. The town fathers are clever, providing unlimited, free bus service to all the major sites and walks in the area. Arosa also offers a 9-hole golf course, clay tennis courts, swimming, boating, fishing and a well-organized Tourist Bureau that sponsors daily morning and evening activities, both cultural and physical. There is a good variety of accommodations—from apartments to 5-star hotels.

2. Engelberg - The picturesque village of Engelberg, at 3,300 ft., is an hour south of Lucerne, tucked into the mountain ranges of central Switzerland. The history of Engelberg is intertwined with the Benedictine Cloister, founded in 1120, which influenced the cultural and religious life over the area in its early years. Now, Engelberg has developed into a leading tourism center for winter skiers and summer walkers. The many beautiful hiking trails have made Engelberg one of the largest year-round resorts in central Switzerland, boasting a particularly effective Tourist Office. The Titlis, a short excursion from Engelberg, stands at 10,000 ft., with a series of lifts, including an innovative, rotating, circular cable car, operating from Stand to Kleine Titlis. Imagine a glass-enclosed cable car, holding 80 people, that rotates as it ascends some 2,000 ft. to reach the top station! The Engelberg Valley, unlike many others in Switzerland, is open, with sunny, terraced meadows filled with grazing cows.

3. Meiringen - The evil Dr. Moriarty, foe of Sherlock Holmes, wrestled with the famous detective on a precipitous mountain ridge, both falling into the craggy depths of Reichenbach Falls. Thus lies the real setting for a fictional character in the resort village of Meiringen. At 1,970 ft., this lovely town sits in a valley divided by the Aare River, rushing to Lake Brienz. The Hasliberg area, at 3,600 ft., overlooks Meiringen on one side, while Reichenbach Falls cascades over the cliffs on the other side. Meiringen is a versatile resort, with many hotels, private apartments and activities—including over 180 miles of marked walking trails. Its central location on the main rail line between Interlaken and Lucerne insures easy access to dozens of excursions and walking options.

ACCOMMODATIONS

The following three-star Swiss hotels are used by the authors on their walking trips. All rooms have private facilities, are comfortable, scrupulously clean and well-located. Most hotels are family-owned and justifiably proud of their kitchens. Consult the "Swiss Hotel Guide," available from the Swiss National Tourist Office, for additional hotel listings.

Champex - Hotel du Glacier-Sporting, 1938 Champex-Lac VS, Switzerland,
Tel: 026 83 14 02, FAX: 83 32 02
Owner - Familie Biseix
Centrally located on the main street, many rooms with balconies overlooking the lake. Swiss buffet breakfast and French-inspired cuisine.

Kandersteg - Chalet-Hotel Adler, 3718 Kandersteg BE, Switzerland,
Tel: 033 75 11 21, FAX: 033 75 19 61
Owner - Familie Fetzer
A cozy and comfortable hotel under the caring eye of Grandma Fetzer, son Andreas and his wife Eija. Centrally located with excellent kitchen and salad buffet at dinner, and full Swiss buffet breakfast. Many rooms with balcony, some modernized with Jacuzzis.

Lauterbrunnen - Hotel Silberhorn, 3822 Lauterbrunnen BE, Switzerland
Tel: 036 55 14 71
Owner - Familie Christian von Allmen
The authors have used this well-located hotel for years. A view of the Lauterbrunnen Valley can be seen from the balconies of most rooms. Excellent Swiss buffet breakfast, outstanding dinners with complete salad bar.

Saas-Fee - Hotel Etoile, 3906 Saas-Fee VS, Switzerland
Tel: 028 57 29 81, FAX: 0 28 57 32 29
Owner - Familie Rolf Bumann

In a quiet part of town, with regional Valais cooking and Swiss breakfast buffet. Many rooms have a balcony overlooking the glaciers.

Samedan - Golf-Hotel des Alpes, 7503 GR, Switzerland
Tel: 082 6 52 62, FAX: 082 6 33 38
Owner - Familie A. Tarnuzzer
Well-located, with owner serving as talented chief chef. Swiss buffet breakfast and excellent regional cooking with salad buffet at dinner. Recently renovated rooms are spacious, some with balconies.

Zermatt - Hotel Bristol, 3920 Zermatt VS, Switzerland
Tel: 028 67 14 75, FAX: 028 67 56 75
Owner - Familie L. Perren-Wyer
Most rooms have balconies with a view of the Matterhorn, and nice ambiance. Swiss buffet breakfast and outstanding kitchen. Away from the touristy main street.

Arosa - Hotel Cristallo, 7050 Arosa GR, Switzerland
Tel: 027 31 22 61, FAX: 027 31 41 40
Owners - Berndt and Heidi Twietmeyer
Large, comfortable, balconied rooms with views of lake and mountains. Full Swiss buffet breakfast—kitchen and ambience outstanding. Centrally located.

Engelberg - Hotel Schweizerhof, 6390 Engelberg OW, Switzerland
Tel: 041 94 11 05, FAX: 041 94 41 47
Owner - Familie Burch-Weibel
A large, restored, grand hotel, located close to the train station, with comfortable rooms, many with balconies. Full Swiss buffet breakfast and dinners.

Meiringen - Sport Hotel Sherlock Holmes - 3860 Meiringen BE, Switzerland
Tel: 036 71 42 42, FAX: 0 36 71 42 22
     Off the main street and bordered by a quiet, tree-lined park. Hotel apartments are modern and spacious, among the best we've seen in Switzerland, although the food and ambiance are less "traditional" than other 3-star hotels.

Index to Walks

Lauterbrunnen

Kandersteg

Samedan

Index

Order Form

For Credit Card ORDERS ONLY - call toll-free
800-669-0773
For Information - call 510-530-0299

To order direct, send check or money order to:
Gateway Books, 2023 Clemens Rd., Oakland, CA 94602

Walking Easy in the Austrian Alps $10.95 . . . $_____
Walking Easy in the Swiss Alps $10.95 . . . . . _____
Where to Retire $12.95 . . . . _____
Choose Mexico $11.95 . . . . _____
Choose Costa Rica $13.95 . . . . _____
Choose Spain $11.95 . . . . _____
Adventures Abroad $12.95 . . . . _____
RV Travel in Mexico $9.95 . . . . _____
Get Up & Go $10.95 . . . . _____
Retirement on a Shoestring $7.95 . . . . _____
The Grandparent Book $11.95 . . . . _____
To Love Again $7.95 . . . . _____

                              Subtotal _____

Postage & Handling
    First Book $1.90 . . . . _____
    Each additional book $1.00 . . . . _____
California residents add 8% sales tax . . . . . _____

                  Total Enclosed $_____

Please ship to:

Name _____

Address _____

City/State/Zip_____
If this is a gift, please let us know if you'd like to include a message.

Our books are shipped bookrate. Please allow 2-3 weeks for
delivery. If you are not satisfied, the price of the book(s) will be
refunded in full. U.S. funds for all orders, please.